In Praise of
Invited: The Ultimate Catholic Wedding Planner

"Where can you find the poetry of the Song of Songs as well as practical preparations for engaged couples entering into marriage? In Stephanie Calis' amazing book, a complete resource for bride and groom!"

— Bill Donaghy, curriculum specialist and teacher,
Theology of the Body Institute

"In a time when fewer Catholics are choosing sacramental marriage, this book charmingly answers the crucial questions of why and how to get married in the Church. *Invited* is the ideal engagement gift for any Catholic couple approaching the altar."

— Karee Santos, co-author of *The Four Keys to Everlasting Love: How Your Catholic Marriage Can Bring You Joy for a Lifetime*

"With a friendly and engaging style, Stephanie Calis provides a wonderfully practical and spiritual guide for all couples preparing for a wedding and a strong marriage."

— Father Joseph Mozer, pastor and
Catholic Engaged Encounter chaplain

D0721204

Invited

THE ULTIMATE CATHOLIC WEDDING PLANNER

STEPHANIE CALIS

Pauline
BOOKS & MEDIA
Boston

Library of Congress Cataloging-in-Publication Data

Calis, Stephanie.
  Invited : the ultimate Catholic wedding planner / Stephanie Calis.
    pages cm
  Summary: "Combines the best of wedding planning guides with the richness of Catholic
faith and practice"-- Provided by publisher.
  ISBN 978-0-8198-3734-9 (pbk.) -- ISBN 0-8198-3734-2 (pbk.) 1. Weddings--Planning.
2. Marriage--Religious aspects--Catholic Church. I. Title.
  HQ745.C34 2016
  392.5--dc23
                              2015034941

Many manufacturers and sellers distinguish their products through the use of trademarks. Any trademarked designations that appear in this book are used in good faith but are not authorized by, associated with, or sponsored by the trademark owners.

The Scripture quotations contained herein are from the *New Revised Standard Version Bible: Catholic Edition,* copyright © 1989, 1993, Division of Christian Education of the National Council of the Churches of Christ in the United States of America. Used by permission. All rights reserved.

Excerpts from the English translation of the *Catechism of the Catholic Church* for use in the United States of America, copyright © 1997, United States Catholic Conference, Inc.— Libreria Editrice Vaticana. Used with permission.

Selections from the *Liturgy of the Word* and the *Catholic Rite of Marriage* copyright © United States Conference of Catholic Bishops. All rights reserved.

Excerpts from papal and magesterium texts copyright © Libreria Editrice Vaticana. All rights reserved. Used with permission.

Cover design by Rosana Usselmann

Cover photo: istockphoto.com/ © wragg

Illustrations by Janelle Bell-Martin

All rights reserved. No part of this book may be reproduced or transmitted in any form or by any means, electronic or mechanical, including photocopying, recording, or by any information storage and retrieval system, without permission in writing from the publisher.

"P" and PAULINE are registered trademarks of the Daughters of St. Paul.

Copyright © 2016, Stephanie Calis

Published by Pauline Books & Media, 50 Saint Pauls Avenue, Boston, MA 02130-3491

Printed in the U.S.A.

www.pauline.org

Pauline Books & Media is the publishing house of the Daughters of St. Paul, an international congregation of women religious serving the Church with the communications media.

1 2 3 4 5 6 7 8 9   20 19 18 17 16

To encounter the mystery [of God] takes patience,
inner purification, silence, and waiting.

— Saint John Paul II,
General Audience, July 26, 2000

This at last is bone of my bones and flesh of my flesh.

— Genesis 2:23

Contents

Introduction

MY FEET HURT. There I stood, minutes away from the start of my wedding Mass, and my last thought as a single woman was how desperately I wished I'd tried on my bridal shoes sooner and returned them for a pair that actually fit. I clutched my dad's arm, hobbling along, and we waited outside the church doors.

Once inside, the aisle was, to my surprise, quite short—certainly shorter than the thirty feet of ramp I'd just walked down to get to the entrance. At the end of the aisle, waiting at the altar, stood my about-to-be husband, radiant with love.

Being engaged and getting married feels a lot like walking down a long ramp in too-small shoes. Sometimes planning your wedding is a huge pain; and your life as husband and wife feels miles away as you inch forward, step after tiny step. Then, when the wedding day arrives, you might find yourself astonished, standing here already, right now, marrying the love of your life and trying to absorb every moment as time passes faster than normal.

In the eighteen months surrounding my wedding, I went to nine other weddings, all of them Catholic and all sublimely beautiful. I loved every minute of witnessing the fulfillment of my friends' vocations. When my turn came, though, I realized I had no clue. *How*, exactly, did one get married in the Catholic Church? There were classes, Mass parts, marriage licenses, locations, plus a long-distance engagement, and all the necessary secular aspects of wedding planning, too.

Miraculously, our wedding was a remarkably peaceful, prayerful day that I carry in my heart. When I found myself unemployed shortly after (the result of following my love to his grad program four hours from my hometown), I had lots of free time to absorb what it meant to be a newlywed and to consider my engaged friends whose own wedding days approached. I noticed few resources available for Catholic brides-to-be. So, my blog, *Captive the Heart*, became a project to provide such a resource and fill my hunger for something creative and productive.

Plenty of great nonreligious wedding planning sources cover everything from dresses to dances to favors, and thank goodness they do. Some excellent guides, in print and online, also offer help for planning a Catholic nuptial Mass and preparing for the sacrament of Marriage. I have noticed, however, that none of these guides combine both of these aspects—the secular *and* the sacred.

Very humbly, then, I present to you this book—my attempt to fill this void and bring together these two sides of wedding planning. In these pages I hope to provide clarity on all the sacramental preparations to be made, from setting a date through walking out of the church, as well as shedding some light on the rest of your to-do list, including registries, dress shopping, and gift giving.

During my engagement, I quickly found out what I was made of: weakness, stress, and mood swings, most of the time. Not exactly a vision of bridal poise. But what's marriage if not a school of love, and what's engagement if not a time to train your heart for the fullness of self-gift you'll give each other at the altar? So, all of my planning advice is framed with the intention of growth in virtue. Getting married, and being married, takes patience, generosity, humility, and fortitude. Through my triumphs and, more often, my errors, I've discovered these virtues can be cultivated in small, habitual ways through countless tasks leading up to your big day. You'll find questions for discussion at the end of each chapter to help you come up with ways to cultivate virtue. My husband also makes an appearance at each chapter's conclusion, offering stories, advice, and reflections from a male perspective, and he later takes the floor in his very own chapter.

Another thing: at the risk of sounding like a lunatic, I really like talking to people about sex. I spent a year as a chastity speaker, my husband and I teach Natural Family Planning to engaged and married couples, and I've developed a deep love for Saint John Paul II's discourses on marriage, sexuality, and salvation known as the theology of the body. I don't intend this book to be a heavy theological explanation of Catholic sexual ethics, but I honestly believe a truthful understanding of sexuality, held in a proper, balanced context within God's design, can heal so many of our wounds and encourage the best, most authentic kind of love. Anything Catholic-wedding-related would be lacking without it. In addition to the basics of planning your wedding, you'll find chapters that get real about sex and who we are as men and women.

And of course, things don't end the minute you leave your wedding reception. They begin. This book concludes with some reflections, born of my discoveries and embarrassing mistakes, on newlywed life.

If you're engaged and reading this, congratulations are in order! There are also, as you've probably found out already, plenty of other things to get in order. The next few pages have two handy, bride-approved checklists to help you organize your ceremony, reception, and budget. Oh, and please, try on your wedding shoes ahead of time. Shall we?

"I Do" To-Dos: A Master Checklist

Practical First Steps

☐ Set up a meeting with your priest to go over dates and preparation requirements.

☐ Sit down with your parents and future in-laws to discuss yours and each family's general expectations regarding who will pay for what.

☐ Decide if you will have a nuptial Mass or the marriage rite outside of Mass.

☐ Set a date.

☐ Set a budget (use the Budget Planning Sheet).

☐ Decide on an approximate guest count.

☐ Identify potential reception venues and schedule phone meetings and visits to learn more.

☐ Choose your bridesmaids, groomsmen, maid of honor, and best man, and invite each of them to be a part of your wedding party.

☐ Send save-the-dates, if you'd like.

Spiritual First Steps

☐ Sign up for a marriage prep program through your parish or diocese, depending on what's offered.

☐ Register for a Natural Family Planning (NFP) course. See Appendix C for resources.

☐ Ask your celebrant to bless your ring and your engagement.

☐ Pray! Ask the Holy Spirit to grant you peace and clarity of mind during this intense time.

Reception Planning

For an in-depth reception to-do list, see the planning sheet in on page 82.

Vendors: Book Your . . .

Note: Some venues include several of these vendors and items, such as food and alcohol, packaged together in the price.

- [ ] Florist
- [ ] Photographer
- [ ] Videographer, if you'd like one
- [ ] Cake baker
- [ ] Caterer, if necessary
- [ ] Bartender
- [ ] DJ or band
- [ ] Transportation

Nuptial Mass Planning

- [ ] Plan your nuptial Mass or ceremony. See the liturgy planning sheet on page 63.
- [ ] Choose and invite your liturgical ministers and other attendants for the Mass or ceremony:
    - [ ] Musicians and vocalists
    - [ ] Readers
    - [ ] Extraordinary ministers of the Eucharist (only at Mass)

- [ ] Altar servers
- [ ] Greeters/ushers
- [ ] Invite any priests whom you'd like to concelebrate the Mass, or deacons to assist.

Attire

- [ ] Go dress shopping! Buy your gown and schedule fittings and alterations.
- [ ] Shop for and buy or rent the groom's suit or tux.
- [ ] Choose dresses and shoes for your bridesmaids, ideally six months or more in advance. Follow up to check that everything's been purchased.
- [ ] Choose suits or tuxes for your groomsmen.
- [ ] Pick out and purchase bridal accessories:

    _____ Shoes

    _____ Jewelry

    _____ Wrap/jacket

    _____ Lingerie

    _____ Purse

4–6 Months in Advance

- [ ] Create a gift registry or set up an online event page to let guests know what you need or want.
- [ ] Browse invitation options and purchase or order them.

- ☐ Book your honeymoon.
- ☐ Arrange for time off from work.
- ☐ Shop for and buy wedding bands.
- ☐ Make or purchase table favors, if favors are desired.
- ☐ Purchase guest sign-in book if you want a record of who attended your wedding and reception.
- ☐ Identify lodging options for out-of-town guests and create a lodging info sheet to include with your invitations.

2–4 Months in Advance

- ☐ Plan your rehearsal dinner:

  _____ Time and place: _____

  _____ Meal: _____

  _____ Guests: _____

  _____ Special items: speeches, gifts, blessings

  _____

  _____

  _____

- ☐ Send thank-you notes for gifts you've received at a shower or other gathering.
- ☐ Purchase gifts for your wedding party and any other important individuals, such as your parents or liturgical ministers, whom you'd like to thank in a special way.

- [ ] Book hair and makeup appointments for the big day, if you want professional services.
- [ ] Mail invitations about eight to twelve weeks in advance of the wedding. Include lodging info for out-of-town guests.
- [ ] Book arrangements for your wedding night.
- [ ] Arrange for any pet care or home sitting during your honeymoon.

1 Month in Advance

- [ ] Apply for your marriage license.
- [ ] Follow up with guests who haven't RSVP'd.
- [ ] Finalize the guest list and make a reception seating chart, if you are assigning tables.
- [ ] Touch base with your vendors and finalize any details.
- [ ] Create a contact sheet for your vendors and wedding party (see the sample sheet in chapter 4).

Wedding Week

- [ ] Finalize rehearsal dinner plans.
- [ ] Confirm transportation and lodging details for out-of-town guests.
- [ ] Pick up reception rentals.
- [ ] Pick up suit rentals or confirm delivery details.
- [ ] Arrange with your vendor floral deliveries for the church, reception venue, and wedding party.

- [ ] Put together a day-of supply kit for the bride and bridesmaids:

  - _____ *Snacks:* Water and high-protein foods like nuts are good!

  - _____ *Beauty:* floss, bobby pins, brush and comb, hair ties, hairspray, nail clippers and file, face wipes, Q-tips, cotton balls, deodorant.

  - _____ *First aid:* bandages, pain relievers, eye drops, hand sanitizer, menstrual products.

  - _____ *Clothes-related:* safety pins, sewing kit, lint roller, stain remover pen, double-sided tape, and blister block for shoes.

- [ ] Distribute the contact sheet to your vendors and wedding party, in person or by e-mail (see page 85).

- [ ] Prepare tips and thank-you notes for your vendors.

- [ ] Pack for your honeymoon.

If You're Changing Your Name

You'll need to change your name on your Social Security card before changing it on any other documents. To do so, bring a certified copy of your marriage license to your nearest Social Security office (find it at SSA.gov) and fill out their application. After your new card arrives, you're free to use it to change your name on your

- [ ] Driver's license
- [ ] Passport
- [ ] Bank accounts

- ☐ Medical records
- ☐ Insurance (medical, car, homeowner, and other)
- ☐ Vehicle registration
- ☐ Leases
- ☐ Loans
- ☐ E-mail address (if you like)

Other Notes:

_____

_____

_____

_____

_____

_____

_____

_____

_____

_____

_____

_____

Budget Planning Sheet

THIS LIST OF expenses has space in each category for you to assign a percentage of your wedding-reception budget. Not sure how to break down costs? As a starting point, you can expect to spend roughly half your budget on reception-related costs (the venue, food and drink, music, and rentals) and can divide the remaining amount according to what you value most. The list is comprehensive, but most likely you won't need every item on it, nor should you feel like you need every item. Obviously, it's your wedding, and you're free to set your budget to include and exclude things however you like. I know expenses add up quickly, so here are a few ways to save.

- A beautiful church doesn't need much decoration, so don't stress about filling it with flowers. Candles alone are gorgeous and inexpensive. If you like, order one or two arrangements for the altar (and, arguably, you could forego these if you're really pinching pennies).

- As you visit potential reception venues and narrow down your options, crunch the numbers with a rough estimate of how many guests you'll have in order to determine whether it's more cost-effective to choose a venue that offers event packages (that is, a meal, decor, and table setups all included) or to rent and order these items individually.

- Skip the full bar and serve only a few varieties of beer and wine.

- Think small, local, and personal for your vendors, and take advantage of your friends' and family members' talents. Instead of a designer-cake bakery, for instance, try the pastry chefs-in-training at the local vocational school. Maybe ask a new photographer who's still growing his or her portfolio to take your engagement photos.

- ◈ Choose flowers that are in season. They generally cost less because they don't have to be imported.

- ◈ Ask a gifted friend to style your hair. Do your own make-up and nails.

- ◈ You don't have to buy all new jewelry and accessories. If your mom, sister, or friend owns a gorgeous piece you love, ask to use it as your "something borrowed."

- ◈ Do you really want to pay for about eight hours' worth of limo service that you get to enjoy for maybe two hours? Consider carpooling with your wedding party to the church and use one of your cars to drive together as husband and wife from the church to the reception.

- ◈ Design and print your own invitations.

- ◈ As a general approach, save wherever you can (use your Top 3 lists to help prioritize which items get the biggest chunk of your budget), but try not to stress about paying for what you really value. For example, if you know you'd go crazy trying to make your own bouquets, even if that were the least expensive option, it's truly worth paying a florist to do it.

Total Budget

Top 3: *List the top three items each of you wants to prioritize most (e.g., photography, music, attire . . .) and use your lists as guidelines for breaking down your budget by category.*

His	Hers
1.	1.
2.	2.
3.	3.

The Mass and Getting Hitched:
_____ % of total budget

Cost	
	Church fee (for having your Mass there)
	Celebrant stipend/donation
	Church décor (e.g., candles or aisle runner, if you'd like them)
	Flower girl and/or ring bearer accessories (e.g., baskets or a ring pillow)
	Marriage prep (e.g., meals and lodging and program fee for an Engaged Encounter weekend)
	NFP course
	Marriage license

The Reception: _____%

Cost	
	Reception venue
	Food
	Alcohol and beverages
	Cake
	Tables
	Chairs
	Serving ware (plates, glasses, utensils)
	Centerpieces
	Favors
	Other (dance floor, lighting, photo booth . . .)
	Gratuities for site POC, wait staff, etc.

Apparel: _____%

Cost	
	Wedding gown
	Suit or tux
	Gown alterations
	Shoes
	Veil
	Lingerie
	Jewelry
	Purse

Beauty: _____%

Cost	
	Hair
	Makeup
	Perfume
	Nails

Paper: _____%

Cost	
	Save-the-date cards
	Invitations
	Mass programs
	Reception place cards
	Thank-you cards
	Stamps

Photography: _____%

Cost	
	Wedding photographer and gratuity
	Engagement photos (if not included in your wedding package)
	Wedding videographer and gratuity

Flowers: _____%

Cost	
	Arrangements for the church
	Bridal bouquet
	Bridesmaids' bouquets
	Groom's and groomsmen's boutonnieres
	Corsages and boutonnieres for parents and grandparents
	Delivery and tip

Music: _____%

Cost	
	Musicians/choir or cantor for nuptial Mass and gratuity
	DJ or reception musicians and gratuity

Gifts: _____%

Cost	
	Bridesmaids
	Groomsmen
	Parents
	Other (Liturgical ministers, friends who pitch in their time or talent)

Transcription: _____ %

Cost	
	Transportation for bride, groom, and wedding party
	Parking
	Gratuity for drivers

Chapter One
First Steps

To my surprise, I didn't want to wear my engagement ring much in the weeks after Andrew proposed—at least not at first. It was about one size too big, and I was petrified of messing it up. I took it off to work out (sweat and the endless scratching potential!), to wash my face (chemicals!), and before going to bed (what if it fell off in my sleep?). We got it sized and that sparkler has rarely left my finger since, with the indentation and perma-tanline to prove it. I truly can't recall the feeling of not having my wedding ring on my hand, nor can I remember much about the whirlwind of giggling and news-sharing that followed our engagement. I clearly *can* remember, however, the thought that constantly popped into my mind: What now?

I didn't have any married friends yet and hadn't been to a family wedding in years, so my knowledge of how to even begin planning was nonexistent. Andrew and I deeply valued a wedding day centered on communion: we were celebrating a sacrament in the Catholic Church, not alone, but in the presence of our family and friends. We hoped our new union as husband and wife could humbly exhibit a living faith to our guests, meeting them wherever they were—the Church and the family are meant to be a communion of persons. Fortunately, that sense of communion also extends to engagement. Assistance from the Church, we discovered, is quite readily available. Here's how we went about planning a Christ-centered day.

The Where and the Whom

First things first: Where are you getting married? Lots of marriage ceremonies take place at hotels, gardens, or historic sites, but the Church requires that Catholic couples marry in, well, an actual church. Why? It's not because the Church is out to rob you of the romantic, oceanfront vows you've always dreamed of. Those sound perfectly nice. But in the eyes of the Church, marriage is more than just *nice*. It's a sacramental reality that literally transforms the couple professing their love and fidelity to one another. Marriage is sacred; it's an act of worship and reverence, and the environment in which it takes place should reflect that. Where is this worship reflected more than in a church, before Jesus—the living God—in the tabernacle?

Weddings are traditionally and most commonly held in the bride's home parish. If, however, another sacred space is meaningful to you and your fiancé, like a shrine or cathedral, it's worth looking into the location's policies for weddings. I had always dreamed of getting married in the beautiful chapel on my college campus, and we did hold our wedding Mass there.

Contacting your parish pastor or campus chaplain shortly after you're engaged will hopefully answer most of your basic

logistical questions about available dates, marriage prep requirements, and other details. If you are close to other deacons or priests,
particularly a spiritual director if you have one, I encourage you to
invite them to your ceremony. Our main celebrant, for instance,
was the pastor from my home parish, who's also been a family
friend for many years. Additionally, we invited Andrew's uncle
and two of our friends who are also priests to concelebrate the
Mass.

A Marriage Ceremony Versus a Nuptial Mass

The Catholic Rite of Marriage can take place on its own. If
either you or your fiancé are not Catholic, celebrating the rite
without a Mass can be respectful for the non-Catholic spouse and
for family members who cannot receive the Eucharist.

More commonly, though (and, in my opinion, even better),
couples elect to celebrate the sacrament of Marriage within a Mass.
True, most marriage ceremonies outside the Church are fairly
short, to the point where an entire liturgy might seem unnecessary
or overly long. If you're feeling this way, I'd encourage you to seek
out resources from your pastor or from Appendix C in this book
that explain the "why" behind the parts of the Mass.

The beauty and the particular significance of nuptial union
(a.k.a. getting married!) are hard to deny. Specifically, each time
Christ becomes present in the Eucharist during the Mass, heaven
and earth, and Jesus and his Church, are united in an intimate way
that transcends time. Love comes to us, in a very tangible way,
through God's grace. Earthly marriage between a husband and
wife is a beautiful icon of this still more beautiful divine marriage.
To me, it's one of the most profound reasons to hold your marriage
ceremony within the context of the Mass.

The When

Everyone's first question about my engagement and impend-
ing plans, I learned, was, "So have you set a date?" The staff at
your ceremony location can provide plenty of information on
availability and scheduling. Andrew and I were surprised to find
churches are frequently just as fully booked as reception venues
nearly every weekend, particularly non-parish churches like the
one at our university. (Ours had a wait list of over a year!) So, if
you have your heart set on getting married at your own college,
for instance, or at your diocese's cathedral, it's wise to inquire
about availability with a spirit of flexibility and set the date based
on the church. If, on the other hand, you're settled on a certain
reception site early on, setting a date based on that site's availability is a smart starting point.

A word about saving the date: couples often get engaged and
then leave it at that for an indeterminate amount of time.
Culturally, men and women are marrying later in life than past
generations, and cohabitation is more commonplace.[1] Although
these trends probably aren't the sole reason for indefinite engage-
ments, I do think they're a contributing factor. If it seems like
there's plenty of time to get married after settling into a career and
post-college social life, and if cohabitation offers some of the inti-
macies of marriage without the full commitment, you might
wonder, "What's the rush?" A few issues arise with this outlook.

First, on a practical level, not much wedding planning can take
place when the engagement is open-ended, particularly with

---

1. Meg Jay, "The Downside of Cohabitating Before Marriage, *The New York
Times*, April 14, 2012. http://www.nytimes.com/2012/04/15/opinion/sunday/
the-downside-of-cohabiting-before-marriage.html.

booking vendors and locations. Choosing a day early on means you can actually begin to plan for it, not just dream about it.

What's more, by setting a date shortly after getting engaged, ideally a date that's not too far off, you're better able to prepare for marriage in a concrete way. I see dating as a more distant preparation for getting married, as you discern marriage with the other person. That's not to say a couple should get engaged the minute they decide they'd like to marry each other—maybe it's during a time in your life, like college, when getting married soon isn't a possibility.

Engagement, on the other hand, is more proximate and in-depth. In my experience, the infinite details of wedding planning brought with them a time of deeper emotional intimacy and preparation for a sacramental reality. At best, an indefinite or very long engagement can be a missed opportunity for preparing your heart. If marriage is still in the distance, having a ring on your finger doesn't feel too different from not having one. At worst, an engagement ring only signifies that a couple won't break up, not that they're actively getting ready for a new phase in their lives. This kind of attitude can create a dead zone where problematic aspects of a relationship go unexamined. When you've found your one and only, shouldn't you feel as if you can't wait to get married, not as if things should just stay status quo?

The Tension . . . Dealing with Tough Family Situations

Your wedding day ultimately comes down to just the two of you. Maybe you're even paying for everything yourselves. And yet, marrying someone unites you not just to your new husband or wife, but to his or her family, for better or worse. Maybe you have complicated relationships with some of your family. Maybe not everyone in your family is Catholic, or maybe you haven't been to Mass in years. I get that big events can certainly bring on high tensions and reopen old wounds. Though some of these aspects might be beyond your control, your own response to them is not.

I encourage you to take these difficulties to prayer, even if you never have before. Give each difficult relationship in your life to Our Lady, and tell her it's all hers. Praying to Mary is like having her personally take your prayers straight to her Son. Who couldn't use that kind of intercession and assistance? By giving each difficulty to her, you lighten your burden, one she will lovingly accept and use for God's glory in some way we can't even fathom. Offer your struggles for something greater: for a long and fulfilling marriage, for your family's sanctification, for healing. Knowing your heartache can be redeemed by the cross means no suffering is meaningless.

Prayer, of course, can be powerful and transforming, which is amazing on a spiritual level. Back on the earthly level, though, I know how rough it can be. Rather than aiming to have every painful situation perfectly resolved, it can be incredibly freeing just to aim for peace in your heart. Be at peace with the fact that any brokenness in your family will never be perfect this side of heaven, nor does it have to be perfected by your wedding day. If something like inviting an estranged family member would cause you more unrest than peace, it's okay to follow the path to your peace over following what etiquette tells you you're supposed to do (assuming doing so won't result in an all-out family war).

Catholic marriage itself can be another source of tension. If you or a family member hasn't practiced the faith for a while, certain guidelines on vows, ceremony music, sex, birth control, and divorce can be tough to understand. If these teachings are hard for you, shelve your pride for just a moment, long enough to look into the reasoning behind the teaching. I love my faith and stand behind the Church 100 percent, but not because I think faith should be blind. The reason I trust so completely is that every time I've questioned a teaching or tradition, it's withstood the test of my logic and objections and proven itself to be intended for our best happiness. And, faith is a gift God grants us—where reason and logic end, faith takes over. But inquire for yourself—talk to a faithful friend or priest about your points of contention, take some time to contemplate their explanations, and aim for a full and humble understanding. Chances are, a deeper understanding of the Church will be hard to write off.

Or, what if you're on board with the Church and someone you're close to isn't? Explaining why, for instance, you and your fiancé aren't writing your own vows or why you're not getting married on a beach takes charity and sensitivity, but it's also an opportunity to meet people where they are, to share the wisdom of the Church, and to break stereotypes about how Christians share their faith. Outside pressure can be hard to deal with, but ultimately, find consolation in knowing that honoring Christ—above all else—on your wedding day will bear so much more fruit than honoring man.

A Spiritual Game Plan

The Master Checklist at the beginning of this book lists a few practical first steps for you as an engaged couple. Consider introducing the following practices to your relationship, starting now.

First, ask for prayers from your friends, your family and future in-laws, and the saints. Intercession is a powerful thing and can flood your relationship with graces throughout the madness.

Second, make a habit of going to Confession, together, regularly (though not at the same time!). During my engagement, I constantly wanted to keep as clean a slate as possible for my now-husband, maybe because I was constantly shorter-tempered with him than I'd ever been before and because our temptations against chastity were stronger than we'd ever experienced. I know how tough going to Confession can be, especially if you haven't received the sacrament in quite some time. Confession is scary. But I promise, even if you think you're going to have a panic attack, the freedom you experience afterward is like nothing else. Nothing. A wellspring of grace flows from the sacraments. Tap into them often. Lastly, if you're the literary type, consider reading a book together on Christian marriage. Appendix C of this book lists plenty of suggestions.

From the Groom

Visuals Versus Vocation

I was unprepared for the number of decisions we had to make when preparing for our wedding. But what I found most difficult was that most decisions seemed unworthy of a serious discussion. It's not that I wasn't invested in our wedding colors. It's just that I genuinely didn't see a significant difference between navy blue and indigo (thanks to Stephanie for supplying an example of not-made-up color names).

I wanted to help, but to me many of the aesthetic decisions weren't big enough to warrant strong opinions. And I don't think that that's a problem. I'm sure one person will care more about how tall the cake stand will be, but what I found most meaningful to our wedding preparation had little to do with aesthetics and very much to do with marrying Stephanie. Of course, the aesthetic parts of a wedding matter, yet they were becoming a distraction from the core of what we were doing: preparing for the total and complete gift of ourselves to each other.

We made a compromise: I'd contribute when I felt strongly about some wedding-related decisions, and the rest of the time I'd contentedly focus on preparing myself to become a husband—a role I'd be entering for the rest of my life.

For Conversation

With your fiancé, list a few words you'd like people to use when describing and remembering your wedding day. Make another list of concrete ways to make it happen.

Thanks to the internet, collecting images and ideas for the picture-perfect wedding is easier than ever. What are the pros and cons of this easy availability? Can you identify ways to reconcile it with a Christ-centered celebration?

With all the logistics involved in planning a nuptial Mass and reception, it can be easy to lose a sense of spiritual planning in your heart. What are a few specific ways to cultivate an inner spiritual life during your engagement?

Many weddings don't take place in a church or follow a ceremonial ritual. What sets apart a marriage in the Church from any other wedding?

Chapter Two
Marriage Prep

Well-intentioned friend: So, how are your wedding plans
  going?

What I said: (breezily) Oh, you know, it's a lot of work,
  but I'm just so excited to marry my best friend!

What I was really thinking: (desperately) Someone please
  tell me *how* to actually get married!

SOUND FAMILIAR? WHEN it came to marriage prep in the
Church, I had engaged friends who talked about things like Pre-
Cana and retreats and meetings with their priest, but it was all
veiled in mystery to me. I thought when it was my turn, all those
abstract things would become more concrete, but I often felt like
they didn't, so I was just blindly guessing. My theory is that everyone gets through it because, odds are, it's the only time she or he
will get married, but wouldn't it be fantastic to have an instruction
manual that just told us how to plan things?

Allow me to present to you my attempt at guidance as you prepare for marriage. It's one thing to just get through a program, and another to actually get something out of it. If you have to do it anyway, putting in the effort to make your marriage prep program worth your time can make the difference between being passive and bored to active and, ahem, engaged. Its richness and benefits might surprise you.

Why Is Marriage Prep Required, Anyway?

When you consider that priests and religious sisters make their vows only after *years* of study and spiritual preparation, married couples have it easy. It might seem like the Catholic Church won't play a daily role in your life after you walk out the doors, the way it would in the life of a priest or sister. In reality, though, the very fact that you're getting married in the Church means it *will* have a bearing on your life, whether or not you intend it.

A marriage in the Church isn't just a wedding. It's a sacramental reality in which bride and bridegroom are transformed by grace, and it's a vocation; a call. On the cross, Jesus gives everything as his body and spirit are entirely broken in the greatest act of love ever known. Blood and water fall from his side onto his mother, the disciple John, and the women weeping below. Christ gives completely, and those who love him receive completely.

That total, emptying self-gift is what spouses are literally called to in marriage. Bleeding and suffering for each other might not sound very sexy, but there's no denying that sacrifice, self-denial, and generosity of heart signify profound, extraordinary love.

Echoing the crucifixion takes virtue. That kind of love takes constant effort that only becomes easier by choosing over and over to put the good of the other first, until it's a habit. As much as we'd like to love that way twenty-four hours a day, virtue doesn't come easy. A solid marriage prep program can provide a foundation for living out authentic, virtuous love. It can pinpoint areas of your relationship that might require extra communication, identify ways to honor God through your marriage and family, and help you get real about matters that might not have come up between you otherwise.

Imaging Cana

It's neither small nor coincidental that Jesus' first public miracle took place at a wedding. If you need a refresher, John's Gospel describes the wedding at Cana:

> On the third day there was a wedding in Cana of Galilee, and the mother of Jesus was there. Jesus and his disciples had also been invited to the wedding. When the wine gave out, the mother of Jesus said to him, "They have no wine." And Jesus said to her, "Woman, what concern is that to you and to me? My hour has not yet come." His mother said to the servants, "Do whatever he tells you." Now standing there were six stone water jars for the Jewish rites of purification, each holding twenty or thirty gallons. Jesus said to them, "Fill the jars with water." And they filled them up to the brim. He said to them, "Now draw some out, and take it to the chief steward." So they took it. When the steward tasted the water that had become wine, and did not know where it came from (though the servants who had drawn the water knew), the steward called the bridegroom and said to him, "Everyone serves the good wine first, and then the inferior wine after the guests have become drunk. But you have kept the good wine until now." Jesus did this, the first of his signs, in Cana of Galilee, and revealed his glory; and his disciples believed in him. (Jn 2:1–11)

Marriage prep in most dioceses is called Pre-Cana, and not only because this part of Christ's ministry is one of the more overt wedding references you'll find in the Bible. There's more to it. First, this is the very first time in John's Gospel that Jesus "manifested his glory." Up until then, Jesus hadn't done anything that revealed himself as the Son of God. The moment when he did was understandably a big deal. It's significant, then, that Jesus chose to reveal his divine nature at a wedding. In doing so, he communicated that marriage has great value and elevated it from a mere union to a *sacrament*, a sign of heavenly grace. The fact that he basically sets up an open bar is just a bonus.

Second, Jesus' mother was there. I picture Mary as a mother bird pushing her baby out of the nest to fly, in spite of the baby never having done it before. "My hour has not yet come," he says. Nope, none of that, she answers. Showtime. Mary's words to the servants are my favorite line from Scripture: "Do whatever he tells you." Her instructions make it plain that she is our mother, too, fully prepared to point us straight in the direction of Jesus. For anyone who says Catholics worship Mary or give her too much praise, I'd challenge them to consider her humility and gentle guidance at Cana. It's not about her. She wants only that her Son's will be done. She desires the good of each wedding guest and, in turn, the good of each of us.

So, a lot can be said for viewing your engagement and marriage prep as your own road to Cana. It's there at the wedding feast that Jesus emphasizes the holiness of marriage, while Mary brings us to Jesus through her intercession. A major transformation occurs. Water becomes wine and Jesus makes his glory known.

In the same way, something is transformed as you say your vows at the altar. Over and over you hear it called the "sacrament of Marriage," but what does that really mean? We can't perceive God's grace with our senses. But the sacraments of the Church make God's grace known to us through something we *can* touch, smell, see, taste, or hear. Think of the water used in Baptism and the bread and wine that become the Eucharist. In marriage, the words of the vows and the consummation of the marriage create an indissoluble bond that transcends earthly promises. Any marriage, in its emotional, physical, and legal bond alone, is no small matter and is respectable on its own. But the eternal, indissoluble bond of a sacramental marriage, set apart by grace, is even more profound.[1]

Choosing a Program

Depending on your diocese or parish, there might be one marriage prep program for all engaged couples, or there might be a few options to choose from. The content is usually the same from program to program within your diocese; it's the formats that differ. If you have a choice, it's worth considering which format might be the best fit for the two of you: if your wedding day is still far off, you might benefit from a weekly program that presents information a little at a time. If your engagement is long-distance, a weekend or one-day retreat might be more convenient. Here's a rundown of what most dioceses offer:

◈ *Multi-week courses:* These Pre-Cana classes are usually taught by a trained married couple and meet over a period

---

1. See Paul Haffner, *The Sacramental Mystery* (Herefordshire, England: Gracewing, 2006), 217.

of weeks or months. They're similar in format to sacramental prep classes you might have had in the past, like for your Confirmation or First Communion. One aspect of marriage prep is discussed per session, such as money, kids, and practicing the faith. You might be given homework in the form of discussion questions and practical ways to apply the topic at hand to your relationship.

❖ *Retreats:* A one-day or weekend course covering the whole gamut at once is a good option if your engagement is long-distance, since it's relatively easy to block a few days out of your schedules in advance. Retreats often feature multiple speakers for different topics, which keeps things interesting, and have plenty of downtime built in for prayer and discussion with just the two of you.

❖ *One-on-one mentoring:* Also known as preparation with a sponsor couple, individual meetings offer a very personal approach, which can be well-suited to couples looking for more than just the basics, or those with unique circumstances like an interfaith marriage. My husband and I chose this option because we knew he'd spend the first five years or so of our marriage in grad school. We wanted to speak with a husband and wife who'd been there, living out marriage and, eventually, babies, with limited income and frequent moves. So our campus chaplain put us in touch with a professor and his wife who had four young kids. Working with a sponsor couple can offer mentoring, friendship, and intercession for your relationship. Who couldn't use more people praying for them?

Don't Just Phone It In

Believe me, I know there are tons of vendors to meet with and envelopes to stuff, and that everyone has an opinion about your wedding, whether you ask for it or not. Who wants to spend an entire day, or even an entire weekend, stuck in a room with even more people telling you how to do things?

Hear me out. If you have to be there anyway, you might as well try to get something out of it. I invite you to open your heart to your marriage prep and put some genuine thought into participation and discussion. Maybe not every single talk will speak to you, but chances are something will. That can only happen when you're disposed to receive, not when you've already made up your mind that none of it matters. My husband and I give talks on sexuality and Natural Family Planning at engaged retreats, which can be anywhere from minimally to maximally awkward. To my surprise, at nearly every talk we've given, I've watched at least one couple in the group go from indifferent to interested by the talk's end, and couples often come up afterward to talk one-on-one. I don't say that to brag about our powers of persuasion. Instead, I see it as a testament to how compelling the material itself is. Church teaching hasn't lasted over two thousand years for nothing.

If I may repeat myself from the previous chapter, I've discovered over time that what seem like rules are, in reality, a roadmap to true happiness and flourishing. They're intended to free us, not keep us down. If a certain teaching doesn't make sense to you, don't be afraid to bring it up. You owe it to yourselves and your relationship to approach your marriage prep with a spirit of inquiry and openness, rather than going in on the defensive. The Holy Spirit works in mysterious ways if you allow it. If a certain topic stirs your heart, don't ignore it! If a married couple on your retreat gives a talk that relates to your own experience or sparks some questions, tell them so. As a speaker, let me personally assure you that meeting couples after a session is one of the best parts of a presentation and is surprisingly un-awkward. I love hearing people's stories, answering questions couples don't want to ask in front of the larger group, and even engaging in respectful debate.

Every marriage prep program aims to be comprehensive, but of course it's not possible to spend ages on each subject or to go as deeply as possible into each one. Chatting with the couples who lead your program, a priest, or a trusted, faithful friend can open up a wealth of resources when you find yourself struggling to understand a particular teaching or thirsting for more. Engage the program leaders in conversation and ask them to point you toward further reading or information. (Appendix C also contains plenty of print and web resources for going deeper.)

Cast Out into the Deep: Getting Personal

Speaking of conversation, it might feel forced during some of your meetings. Exercises like reading questions from a piece of paper and asking them to each other, perhaps within earshot of other couples who are probably strangers, isn't the most natural mode of speaking.

Consider, though, the underlying purpose of all these exercises: to foster honest talk between you and your fiancé and to bring to light issues you might not have thought about before. You'll get out of your program what you put into it, so move across the room where no one can hear you, fight through the self-consciousness, and strive to be candid and unguarded.

Since you're getting married, it's likely the two of you have talked at least a little about personal matters. That might include things like debt, wounds from past relationships, or how you envision your marriage and family life. If you've also brought up your thoughts on money, children, and how you'll make big life decisions, way to go—it can be surprisingly easy to get along perfectly well, yet never talk much about these serious matters.

Now's the time to do that. A good Pre-Cana program is intended to help you work through things that don't come up on a daily basis, and to come to a deeper sense of self-knowledge and knowledge of your spouse-to-be. That's why it pays to be completely honest and understanding, seeking peace between you above all else, even when it's uncomfortable.

Case in point: when Andrew and I talked about his strong preference that our children be homeschooled, I'd panic, imagining a lifetime of homeschooling stereotypes and feeling like I was on house arrest. How, I wondered, could we feel so right for each other, yet disagree over one of the most important aspects of our future family? We eventually realized that coming to an identical, final opinion on every aspect of our relationship and its future wasn't a prerequisite for getting married. That would be boring, and also impossible. Our children's education hadn't even come to pass yet; neither, for that matter, had our actual children. Someday we would make those choices, bearing in mind what's best for each other and our family, for that particular time.

The point of all these discussions was to learning how to deal with our differing opinions in a constructive, loving way. Remind yourselves often that marriage prep doesn't exist to make you feel bad about your flaws or make you question your compatibility. Rather, it highlights previously unprobed aspects of your relationship and guides you in productive, self-giving ways to resolve problems and differences.

To See the Face of God

Our sponsor couple told us something beautiful that I still think about often: you can never fully know another person's soul, yet marriage is an opportunity to constantly know the one you love more deeply and completely.

Time has proven them absolutely right. I still find myself smiling like crazy, the way I did when we first started dating, when I suddenly learn something new about Andrew. Every once in a while, we make a game of trying to tell each other stories we've never told before. Getting engaged, getting married, and becoming parents has revealed to us new parts of who we are.

Maybe most amazingly of all, these experiences have revealed us to ourselves. There's a line from the musical *Les Misérables* that says loving another person is like seeing the face of God. I fully believe my husband's love has not so much changed me as it has made me more and more who I am, in the way God created me. Falling in love, we've seen, doesn't reach a certain point and then cease. It's continual. What a grace.

✦ *From the Groom* ✦

Bringing Your Marriage Prep from the Classroom to Your Daily Lives

I highly recommend going on a date after your engaged retreat or after each marriage prep session. Chances are, the material you've just taken in will come up in your conversation over dinner or during a walk, and it won't feel like you are forcing yourselves to talk about it. Plus, dates are an important opportunity to focus on each other and get a respite from all the challenges—both spiritual and practical—of marriage prep.

◈ *For Conversation* ◈

If you have yet to attend a Pre-Cana course, what are your expectations? Discuss any anticipation or concerns you might be feeling. If you've completed your program, how did it compare to your expectations? If any particular topic still resonates in your mind, list ways to continue pursuing and learning about it.

Read and meditate together on the Wedding at Cana (see Jn 2:1–11). Talk about passages that stand out to you. Identify concrete ways to invite Jesus and Mary into your marriage.

Why do you think personal matters like budgeting, sexuality, and core beliefs are so hard to talk about sometimes? Identify a few ways you and your fiancé can open up on these matters as you prepare for marriage.

Charles Dickens wrote, "a wonderful fact to reflect upon, that every human creature is constituted to be that profound secret and mystery to every other."[2] What new discoveries have you made about each other as you prepare for marriage? How have they changed you?

---

2. Charles Dickens, *A Tale of Two Cities* (London: J. M. Dent & Sons Ltd. Everyman's Library, 1906), 9.

Chapter Three
Planning Your Nuptial Mass

LET'S GET ONE thing clear. I have no delusions of replacing or competing with the hundreds of wedding planning, etiquette, and inspiration resources out there. Instead, I hope you'll find this chapter a helpful supplement to those resources, particularly when it comes to your wedding liturgy. Additionally, though I certainly hope getting hitched goes off without a hitch, I also hope even the most unexpected wedding-day catastrophes don't steal your joy.

And believe me, there is so much joy on tap. At every Mass, when bread and wine become the very Body and Blood of Christ, Jesus' complete, self-emptying love becomes real to us like nothing else. In the Eucharist, Jesus gives us that gift of himself and his love and dwells within us.

As amazing as all that is, I get that planning a Mass and reception is, well, wildly stressful. The simplest way to calm down? Remember your wedding is only one day. A huge one, yes, and one that deserves all the planning and organizing efforts you're putting in, but one day just the same. Your marriage is a lifetime. Stay focused on the sacrament, look forward not just to the big day but the day after that, and the day after that, and cultivate a deep understanding of love, and you can just be.

Love Is a Verb

You're getting married. Naturally, you love each other. What does that mean, and what does it look like? My high school self teared up over dozens of passionate kisses, slow dances under the stars, and public serenades in movies, and I eagerly awaited that kind of romance for myself. As I got older, I started seeing those gestures as sweet in a cinematic sort of way, but less romantic and real than I had in the past. I started finding romance, instead, in two individuals suffering for one another, in sacrifice, in vulnerability. What was it that changed in my heart?

I like to think it wasn't that I became sadder or more cynical about relationships ("Baby, I love you. You make me suffer like no one else."). The difference I came to notice between breezy rom-com love and the deeper love I'd started to crave was intention. It does require effort to dash to the airport before the man of your dreams takes off forever, or to hold a boom box over your head outside your girlfriend's window, but those acts are meant to provoke feelings. Authentic, lasting love involves something more: it's an act of the will. It's the choice to put the good of the other before yourself, time and again, even at the cost of your own preferences. Practicing sacrifice brings virtue and, in fact, greater joy. Because of love, you might come to actually *want* to put your own free will aside out of love for the other.[1] Love is a verb, not an emotion.

Never Gonna Give?

Loving selflessly is no small task. Husbands and wives are called to love the way Christ does on the cross, giving themselves completely to each other and withholding nothing. Frankly, it's really, really hard. Marriage is purification in love, yet purification is also a process.

I first encountered this vision of love as self-gift on a retreat where the only person I knew was my college boyfriend. I was amazed, but also freaked out. I could never live up to that perfection, I thought, so I concluded I should probably just give up and accept that I was doomed never to get married due to failure at love. But wait. In Latin, the word *perfect* is defined as "finished" or "complete." So it's no wonder we can't love flawlessly this side of heaven, because as long as we walk this earth, we're never the finished versions of ourselves. Not yet. Jesus himself doesn't say, "It is finished" until he takes his last breath at Calvary (see Jn 19:30).

Meanwhile, be kind to yourselves. We're inundated with false images of love every day, making it even harder than it already is to love authentically, let alone effortlessly. Rick Astley's 1987 hit, "Never Gonna Give You Up," is one of the false ones. You know

---

1. See Edward Sri, *Men, Women, and the Mystery of Love: Practical Insights from John Paul II's Love and Responsibility* (Cincinnati: Servant Books, 2007), 60.

the words: he's never gonna let his woman down, never make her cry, never hurt her . . .

Never gonna let her down? Even in the happiest, most well-adjusted relationships, expectations like these aren't realistic. Compare Rick's promises to the language of wedding vows:

> *I promise to be true to you in good times and in bad;*
> *in sickness and in health.*
> *I will love you and honor you all the days of my life.*

Your vows don't seal off your relationship from difficulty, let alone guarantee you'll never fight. They do, however, promise the most faithful love—the kind of love that doesn't cease when your baby cries at 2:00 AM or when you suddenly have to empty your savings account. It's a love you can trust and count on even in the moments your emotions just aren't on board.

So instead of viewing the fullness of Christ-like, lay-your-life-down love as an unattainable ideal you can't even hope to compete with, I suggest seeing it as the most beautiful, *perfect* model of love imaginable. Model your marriage after the Cross, not after hilariously bad pop songs, and watch both your will to love and your love itself continually strengthen. Speaking of which, the moment when bread and wine are transformed into Jesus' Body and Blood take you straight back to Calvary at every Mass.

Planning Your Nuptial Mass

The great thing about a Catholic nuptial Mass (aside from the real presence of Jesus in the Eucharist) is that because the Mass is the prayer of the Church, the language of the liturgy is already written and almost entirely planned for you. It's literally in God's hands. On a practical level, this makes things easier (you only need to show up at Mass, and you don't need to design your own wedding ceremony). Yet something deeper is going on than just convenience. On the spiritual level, you're united with the entire Body of Christ, the Church, each time you attend Mass and receive the Eucharist. And during *this* particular Mass, the two of you are entering into a sacrament, bearing God's love to everyone present to witness it. Together you're taking part in a moment of "beauty ever ancient, ever new."[2]

Since it is your wedding Mass, though, some aspects of the liturgy are personally chosen by the bride and groom.

Liturgical Ministers

Chapter One details identifying a priest to celebrate your Mass. You're also free to designate other individuals as readers, extraordinary ministers of the Eucharist (bear in mind that these individuals, particularly Eucharistic ministers, may have to be trained and commissioned if they have never done these ministries before), altar servers, gift-bearers, and musicians. So whom to choose?

I encourage you to give your choice of liturgical ministers some deep thought. Obviously, inviting someone to take part in your day, whether as a bridesmaid, groomsman, or otherwise, says you value the relationship you share and that you'd like to honor them with a special role. Getting married in the Church means these invitations carry additional weight.

Every Mass brings a taste of heaven to us on earth through Jesus' Body and Blood. Nuptial Masses are no different. By extension, each individual involved in the Mass bears the responsibility

---

2. Saint Augustine, *Confessions* (New York: Penguin, 1961), 211.

of conveying that sacredness to everyone attending. So, when choosing liturgical ministers, consider whether they'll treat the Mass, and the day in general, with the reverence it deserves. Have they been to church lately? Will they be drunk at the reception in a few hours? I completely understand the sincere desire to share your wedding with the important people in your life. If certain people you love don't seem like the best fit for a role in the Mass itself, you can invite them to be greeters, ushers, or to share a special dance with you at your reception.

Choosing Readings

Nuptial Masses follow the same order as the Liturgy of the Word during a Sunday Mass: a first reading from the Old Testament, followed by a responsorial psalm, and then a second reading from the New Testament, and then the Gospel. The United States Conference of Catholic Bishops (USCCB) provides an approved series of readings, but how to choose? Maybe you've been planning this aspect of your wedding for years, or maybe you've never heard of some of the selections. I encourage you to read over the options together and see what speaks to your hearts. Even if it takes some time to familiarize yourselves with the selections and agree on them, reading Scripture together can only benefit your relationship—it's hard to argue when your Bible's open.

Having been to almost a dozen Catholic weddings in about four years, I consider myself well-versed in the wedding readings category. Surprisingly, there were hardly any repeats among these profoundly beautiful, holy liturgies. I learned at some point that if you prefer, and if your priest approves, you can choose alternate readings from the ones suggested by the USCCB. At one wedding, the couple chose for their Gospel reading John's account of

Jesus' passion. During the homily, the priest made the point that although the long, bloody crucifixion isn't necessarily the prettiest image (far from it!), Jesus' laying down of his life for his bride, the Church, is the ultimate vision of married love. The beauty of that image brought me to tears. So if another passage is particularly meaningful to you as a couple, it's worth asking permission to use it for your Mass.

Selections for the Liturgy of the Word [3]

Work your way through these passages together, asking the Holy Spirit to make you vessels of God's word as you choose your readings.

First Reading—Old Testament

1. Male and female he created them (Genesis 1:26–28, 31a).

2. At last, bone of my bones and flesh of my flesh (Genesis 2:18–24).

3. Marriage of Isaac and Rebekah (Genesis 24:48–51, 58–67).

4. Marriage of Tobiah and Sarah (Tobit 7:6–14).

5. Wedding prayer of Tobiah and Sarah (Tobit 8:4b–8).

6. The woman who fears the Lord is to be praised (Proverbs 31:10–13, 19–20, 30–31).

---

3. See *Planning a Catholic Wedding: Readings*, copyright © United States Confraternity of Catholic Bishops, http://www.foryourmarriage.org/old-testament-readings/.

7. Set me as a seal on your heart (Song of Songs 2:8–10, 14, 16a; 8:6–7a).

8. Blessed the husband of a good wife (Sirach 26:1–4, 13–16).

9. I will place my law within them, and write it upon their hearts (Jeremiah 31:31–32a, 33–34a).

Responsorial Psalm

The following list is the text of the assembly's response.

1. The earth is full of the goodness of the Lord (Psalm 33:12 and 18, 20–21, 22).

2. I will bless the Lord at all times *or*
   Taste and see the goodness of the Lord (Psalm 34:2–3, 4–5, 6–7, and 8–9).

3. The Lord is kind and merciful *or*
   The Lord's kindness is everlasting to those who fear him (Psalm 103:1–2, 8 and 13, 17–18a).

4. Blessed the man who greatly delights in the Lord's commands *or*
   Alleluia (Psalm 112:1bc–2, 3–4, 5–7a, 7b–8, 9).

5. Blessed are those who fear the Lord *or*
   See how the Lord blesses those who fear him (Psalm 128:1–2, 3, 4–5).

6. The Lord is compassionate toward all his works (Psalm 145:8–9, 10 and 15, 17–18).

7. Let all praise the name of the Lord *or*
   Alleluia (Psalm 148:1–2, 3–4, 9–10, 11–13a, 13c–14a).

Second Reading—New Testament

1. What will separate us from the love of Christ? (Romans 8:31b–35, 37–39).

2. Offer your bodies as a living sacrifice, holy and pleasing to God (Romans 12:1–2, 9–18 [long form], or Romans 12:1–2, 9–13 [short form]).

3. Let each of us please our neighbor for the good (Romans 15:1b–3a, 5–7, 13).

4. Your body is a temple of the Holy Spirit within you (1 Corinthians 6:13c–15a, 17–20).

5. Love is patient, love is kind (1 Corinthians 12:31–13:8a).

6. This is a great mystery, but I speak in reference to Christ and the Church (Ephesians 5:2a, 21–33 [long form], or Ephesians 5:2a, 25–32 [short form]).

7. Rejoice in the Lord always (Philippians 4:4–9).

8. Put on love, that is, the bond of perfection (Colossians 3:12–17).

9. I will never forsake you or abandon you (Hebrews 13:1–4a, 5–6b).

10. Be of one mind, sympathetic, loving toward one another, compassionate, humble (1 Peter 3:1–9).

11. Those who keep his commandments remain in him, and he in them (1 John 3:18–24).

12. Beloved, let us love one another, because love is of God (1 John 4:7–12).

13. Blessed are those who have been called to the wedding feast of the Lamb (Revelation 19:1, 5–9a).

Gospel Reading

1. The Beatitudes (Matthew 5:1–12a).

2. You are the salt of the earth. . . . You are the light of the world (Matthew 5:13–16).

3. Everyone who listens to these words of mine and acts on them will be like a wise man who built his house on rock (Matthew 7:21, 24–29 [long form], or Matthew 7:21, 24–25 [short form]).

4. What God has joined together, man must not separate (Matthew 19:3–6).

5. Love the Lord, your God . . . love your neighbor as yourself (Matthew 22:35–40).

6. A man shall leave his father and mother and be joined to his wife, and the two shall become one flesh (Mark 10:6–9).

7. The wedding feast at Cana (John 2:1–11).

8. Love one another as I love you (John 15:9–12).

9. No one has greater love than this, to lay down one's life for one's friends (John 15:12–16).

10. That they may be brought to perfection as one (John 17:20–26 [long form], or John 17:20–23 [short form]).

Choosing Music

Wedding music can range from traditional hymns and classical selections to newer praise and worship songs; the choice is yours. Who's going to play it, and how do you choose from the hundreds of songs in the hymnal? Many parishes have a wedding coordinator or administrative assistant who can help you find musicians and singers. You might consider singers and instrumentalists from the parish choir, friends or family members who sing and play, or student choral or instrumental groups from local universities or community colleges.

A nuptial Mass includes all the musical selections you would hear at any Mass, plus a processional song and a selection for the entrance of the bride. You'll also choose a responsorial psalm, to be sung between the first and second readings, and the arrangements you prefer for the parts of the Mass, that is, the Alleluia and acclamation after the consecration. When selecting music for the Mass parts, it can be beneficial to choose musicians who have experience with Catholic weddings.

For the ease of your planning and for some inspiration, here's a rundown of the order of the Mass and a few musical suggestions to get you started, ranging from true-blue traditions to more original choices. A violinist who has played at dozens of weddings shared with me that musicians usually don't have much time to rehearse or learn new songs before the big day, so show them your gratitude by giving them advance notice of your choices!

Wedding Procession

SUGGESTED SELECTIONS

Canon in D Major (J. Pachelbel)

Jesu, Joy of Man's Desiring (J. S. Bach)

"Rondeau" from *Abdelazer Suite* (H. Purcell)

Entrance of the Bride

SUGGESTED SELECTIONS

"Be Thou My Vision" (D. Forgaill)

"Come Thou Fount of Every Blessing" (R. Robinson)

"Sanctuary" (J. Thompson)

Entrance Hymn

SUGGESTED SELECTIONS

"Holy God, We Praise Thy Name" (I. Franz)

"All Creatures of Our God and King" (Francis of Assisi, William H. Draper)

"Love Divine, All Loves Excelling" (C. Wesley)

"Holy Is the Lord" (C. Tomlin)

Presentation and Preparation of the Gifts

SUGGESTED SELECTIONS

"Litany of the Saints" (Various arrangements)

"Set Me as a Seal" (M. Maher)

"Alabaster" (Rend Collective)

"Make Me a Channel of Your Peace—Prayer of Francis" (Francis of Assisi, S. Temple)

Communion Hymn

SUGGESTED SELECTIONS

"How He Loves" (J. McMillan)

"It Is Well With My Soul" (H. Spafford, P. Bliss)

"Garden" (M. Maher)

"*Panis Angelicus*" (T. Aquinas, C. Franck)

"Let All Mortal Flesh Keep Silence" (R. Williams)

"Hungry" (K. Scott)

Dedication to the Blessed Mother

SUGGESTED SELECTIONS

"*Ave Maria*" (Schubert)

"As I Kneel Before You" (M. Parkinson)

Recessional

SUGGESTED SELECTIONS

"Joyful, Joyful, We Adore Thee" (L. Beethoven, H. Van Dyke)

"O God Beyond All Praising" (G. Holst)

"Your Grace Is Enough" (M. Maher)

"Everlasting God" (B. Brown)

Why Frank Sinatra Can't Walk You Down the Aisle, And Why You Can't Write Your Own Vows

Music has such evocative power, particularly when you have a favorite memory or emotion attached to a piece, and what better time than your wedding to break out the love songs? The Church respectfully requests that you reserve non-religious music for your reception instead of your Mass. It's not because secular music is bad, but because it doesn't fit the context of the occasion. You don't sing the national anthem, for instance, at a birthday party instead of "Happy Birthday," though both songs express themes of celebration and honor.

In the same way, both secular and religious wedding songs express love and the joy of your union, yet the context matters. The Mass is a sacred occasion. As such, the music accompanying it should have a sacred purpose in mind: worship, petition, or adoration. Since your marriage is taking place in the Church, therefore, the music for the liturgy should be written specifically for the Church. I was surprised to learn Wagner's "Bridal Chorus" (a.k.a. "Here Comes the Bride") is generally not permitted for Catholic liturgies because it was written as a theater piece, not a song of worship. It is from the opera *Lohengrin*, and contextually it "actually accompanies the couple to the bedroom, not the altar!"[4]

Similarly, getting married in the Church means speaking the words of the Church. The language of your wedding vows isn't arbitrary. When the bride and groom say them, in the presence of

---

4. "Wedding Topics: The Catholic Wedding Procession," Catholic Wedding Help (2008). http://www.catholicweddinghelp.com/topics/wedding-proces sion.htm.

witnesses, the couple is conferring a sacrament on each other, literally transforming their bond into something eternal. Christ, in turn, confers grace on them.

In every sacrament, words matter. For example, the sacraments of Reconciliation and the Eucharist are considered valid only when the words of absolution and consecration, respectively, are spoken exactly according to their prescribed rites. In the same way, a major part of rendering your marriage valid in the eyes of the Church is adhering to the language of the sacrament as you speak the words of consent and then your vows. But that doesn't mean you can't creatively profess your love to each other in different settings. Prepare a short speech or toast to your new spouse for the reception, or write each other letters to exchange before you walk up the aisle.

Dedication to Our Lady: *Ad Jesu, Per Mariam* [5]

Mary is the ultimate bride: humble, pure, filled with the Holy Spirit, and seeking only the Father's will. She is worthy of all our love, yet Catholics don't worship her or substitute her for God. Instead, Mary hears our prayers and presents them to Jesus with joyful intercession. She "renders captive the heart of man to deliver him over to her Divine Son."[6] If you want to get close to Jesus, get close to his Mother.

That said, it's traditional for the bride and groom to spend a few moments after Communion praying to Our Lady to bless their marriage. As easy as it is to just plunk down a bouquet in front of a

---

5. This is translated "To Jesus, through Mary."
6. Fulton Sheen, *Three to Get Married* (New York: Scepter, 1996), 129.

Mary statue or altar and say a Hail Mary, I encourage you to genuinely talk with her. Ladies, ask her to show you what it is to be a
wife and mother and how to receive the love of your husband.
Men, ask her to teach you how to love a woman. In a way, the dedi-
cation to Mary is one of the most intimate parts of your wedding
Mass. All eyes are on you, yet the two of you have your backs to the
congregation, and no one else will be able to hear what you're saying. Savor the moment, one of your first as husband and wife, and
invite Our Lady into your married life.

Your Rehearsal and Its Dinner

By the time your rehearsal dinner rolls around, nearly all of your
preparation is done. So you can just relax, let someone else tell you
what to do and where to stand, and enjoy a meal with the people you
love. Traditionally, the groom's family hosts, and the evening can be
as fancy as a multi-course restaurant meal or as simple as a backyard
barbecue and bonfire. One of the most fun rehearsal dinners I ever
attended was just beer and chicken wings at the bar in my college
town—nobody has to break the bank to have a great evening.

It's thoughtful, though certainly not required, to invite out-of-
town guests to the dinner and to extend some gesture of welcome.
I'm not talking swag bags brimming with artisan water and fancy
toiletries, unless you want them. A quick note saying hello, along
with directions to convenience stores, your favorite area restaurants, and the church—maybe with a small snack—is perfect.

I was surprised how quickly the actual wedding rehearsal was
over before we were off to the dinner. Consider it a night off from
all your planning and just bask in the presence of your families and
wedding party—tomorrow at your reception, quality time with
each guest will feel much harder to come by. Don't forget at this

time to give any gifts to your bridesmaids, groomsmen, the celebrant, and your parents. If you're inclined, it's also gracious for you
and your fiancé to address your rehearsal dinner guests with a
quick, informal speech expressing your thanks.

In addition to welcoming your guests and thanking everyone
who will be standing next to you, the night before the wedding
also presents you with a unique spiritual opportunity. Consider
building time into the agenda for a few of the following:

- Ask your priest to hear you and your fiancé's confessions at
  the conclusion of the rehearsal (you can invite your family and wedding party members to go to Confession, as
  well). Entering into marriage with a freshly purified soul,
  absolved from all sin, disposes the two of you to receive
  the fullest graces of the sacrament. You might also consider asking the priest to hear confessions for your guests
  during the hour before the nuptial Mass begins.

- Your wedding party has the potential to be so much more
  than the people who walk up the aisle with you and circle
  around during your first dance. By taking part in your
  wedding Mass, they, along with the entire congregation,
  are expressing their consent and support for your marriage. They take on the responsibility of interceding for
  your relationship. Spend some time in prayer with them
  before heading to dinner and before the nuptial Mass.
  At the moment of the consecration during the Mass,
  Jesus' Body and Blood are truly made present as the priest
  elevates the host and we revere Christ among us. Eucharistic adoration takes that singular moment and sustains
  it, exposing the consecrated host for us to gaze upon and
  pray in the real presence of Jesus. Ask your priest to lead

a holy hour for you and your wedding party by arranging
for Eucharistic adoration, maybe along with some praise
and worship, to conclude the evening.

⬥ Steal time for some solitude and prayer in your final moments as an unmarried couple. Go on a Rosary walk, asking Mary to pray for your marriage, offer up some off-the-
cuff prayers together, share one last unmarried kiss, and
trade letters to read while getting ready for the wedding.

──────────── ⬥ *From the Groom* ⬥ ────────────

Crowd Your Heart, Not Your Planner

I am a man who likes my day planner. I enjoy the feeling of
checking things off, and I hate the feeling of leaving them unfin-
ished or ignored. With all the preparations for our wedding and
the Mass, I had many things to happily check off my list, but new
obligations appeared more quickly than my check-off-loving self
preferred. Even on the night of the rehearsal, I felt like we would
never finish everything that still needed to be done.

Completely overwhelmed by the practical side of a wedding, I
had been significantly ignoring the spiritual part. At our rehearsal,
we were able to have the priest hear our confessions, and we stayed
afterward to pray in front of the tabernacle before heading to dinner. During my prayer, I rejoiced that I was kneeling beside the
woman who would be my wife in a matter of hours, focused on how
wonderful it was to be marrying Stephanie—the person who knows
my heart better than anyone. While I knew important, practical,
wedding-related things were calling for my attention, this was a
chance to put them in God's hands, ask for his help, and push them

(at least temporarily) out of my mind. I wanted to get out of my head to consider all the wonders that were crowding my heart.

◈ *For Conversation* ◈

Talk about your favorite romantic moments in movies, songs, or literature (gentlemen, I know you have one). Identify what it is about these moments that pull on your heart. What's at their root (e.g., feelings, sacrifice, duty, honesty)?

Read over the Catholic Rite of Marriage, particularly the vows, in Appendix A. Spend time discussing what, exactly, your promises will mean, and what they'll look like in the day-to-day of your married life.

Why does it matter to have liturgical music instead of pop music at your Mass, and that the bride and groom use the Church's wording for their vows?

What's your relationship with Mary? If you don't really have one, you can start today. Consider making prayer to her a part of your marriage prep. Ask her intercession for the good of your relationship and for the grace to live out your wedding vows each day.

Once again, spend some time reading over the suggested passages for your wedding readings. Use the worksheet that follows to help plan your nuptial Mass.

Order of the Mass Planning Sheet for Readings and Music

INTRODUCTORY RITES

Processional music

Selection _____

Entrance of the bride

Selection _____

Greeting

Gloria

Selection _____

Collect (Opening Prayer)

LITURGY OF THE WORD

First Reading

Selection _____

Responsorial Psalm

Selection _____

Second Reading

Selection _____

Gospel Acclamation (Alleluia)

Selection _____

Gospel

Selection _____

Homily

RITE OF MARRIAGE

Address and statement of intentions

Consent and exchange of vows

Blessing and exchange of rings

Prayer of the Faithful

LITURGY OF THE EUCHARIST

Presentation and Preparation of the Gifts

Selection _____

Eucharistic Prayer

Preface Acclamation ("Holy, Holy . . .")

Selection _____

Memorial Acclamation

Selection _____

Great Amen

Selection _____

COMMUNION RITE

The Lord's Prayer

Nuptial Blessing

Sign of Peace (you might be invited to kiss now . . .)

Lamb of God

Selection _____

Communion

Selection _____

CONCLUDING RITES

Final Blessing (or kiss now!)

Dismissal

Recessional

Selection _____

Chapter Four
Planning Your Reception

ANDREW, DESCRIBING HIS best friend's wedding, said, "The Mass was transcendent, and the reception was killer." Not a bad goal. I want to touch on the basics of reception-planning in light of striking that exact balance—that is, being radiant witnesses to Christ's love while enjoying the party of a lifetime. At the end of the chapter, you'll find a handy reception-planning worksheet and day-of contact sheet. But first, let's talk about the celebrations leading up to the big day.

Bachelor and Bachelorette Parties: Getting Real

Just say the words "bachelor" and "bachelorette" and booze, reality TV, inappropriate cakes, and *The Hangover* come to mind. Our culture tends to view marriage as a radical divide in one's life, after which youth and freedom are no longer acceptable excuses for bad decisions. To be free, though, doesn't mean you have license to do whatever you want. Freedom is the capacity to choose between goods. Saint John Paul II said, "Freedom is for love."[1] That is, when you love someone, you don't just place their happiness and well-being before your own because you're supposed to. You do it because love makes you actually *want* to put your beloved first.

Your entire dating and engaged relationship has been an education in learning to intentionally love the other person more than you love yourself. Why suspend your efforts for a few hours right before you tie the knot? I challenge you to be countercultural: ditch the sleazy bachelor and bachelorette parties.

Does that mean you should have a completely dry, Puritan-themed party? No way. The Dominican priest Dominic Prummer was right on when it comes to enjoying a few beverages: "It's okay to drink," he said, "to the point of hilarity."[2] Beyond that point, drunkenness surrenders your faculties and produces a false reality. Why would that be more appealing than your actual reality, that is, preparing to marry the love of your life? Staying sober enough to hold onto your good judgment is a way to be real. It says you respect yourself and have the confidence to be accountable for your decisions. Getting drunk on purpose is inauthentic.

Inviting strippers isn't authentic either, nor does it reflect the commitment you'll soon be making at the altar. If on any other day in your lives, another man or woman flirted with your fiancé,

1. Karol Wojtyla, *Love and Responsibility* (Boston: Pauline Books & Media, 2013), 98.

2. See Dominic Prummer, OP, *Manuale Theologia Moralis: Secundum Principia S. Thomae Aquinatis*, Vol. II.

danced for him or her while practically naked, or grabbed his or her butt, I assume you'd have something to say about it. So why would you feel differently if that man or woman were a stripper? The only way to feel okay with it is to dehumanize them, reducing them to a collection of body parts. Every human person is so much more than just a body and its parts. Everyone deserves to be seen with respect, even (and perhaps especially) strippers. Honor yourself, your fiancé, and your future marriage, and honor the human dignity of sex workers by refusing to partake of their services. Spend the days before your wedding doing something other than looking at other men's and women's bodies.

That being said, how can you celebrate your wedding week with your friends in a clean way that's not lame? Some original and memorable options might be:

- exploring (staying overnight in a city that is new to you, camping, picnicking);

- sampling (a beer, wine, chocolate, olive oil, or cheese tasting);

- crafting (a jewelry, painting, or pottery studio);

- moving (dance lessons, a 5K or obstacle run, visiting an old-school arcade);

- soaking up some culture (the theater, the movies, the ballpark); and

- treating yourselves (massages, manicures, a blow-dry bar).

Choosing a Venue

Hopefully, by the time you're heading out to your bachelor and bachelorette parties, your reception planning is almost complete. But to get to that point, you've first got to start some-where. Step one is choosing a site for your reception.

All the bridal magazines and websites I immersed myself in gave me irrational anxiety that every venue in town would be booked already if I didn't make reservations the second the engagement ring was on my finger. I *do* think booking your reception should be a top priority after you set a date, along with getting the church and marriage prep logistics in order with your celebrant (reread the section on "The When" in Chapter 1 for more on determining whether booking the church or booking the reception site first makes the most sense for you). But before rushing to put down a deposit, take some time to consider what sort of atmosphere you and your fiancé want to aim for and what you can afford. Ask yourselves if you'd like your reception to be indoors or outdoors, formal or informal, and how many guests you'll have.

Even when you're familiar with the town where you'll be mar-ried and some of the event venues it has to offer, it's overwhelming enough to figure out what's available to you, let alone choose one. As you hone in on the ambience you have in mind, how do you find a reception site that matches what you're imagining? Some great resources for getting started include:

- The office staff at your church (some parishes even have a wedding coordinator that helps make sure things run smoothly on the big day);

- Your wedding photographer—even if you haven't booked one yet, many photographers have blogs with photos from their most recent events, along with location details;

- Facebook groups for brides in your area.

Consider researching:

- Your parish hall. It might not sound terribly fancy, but don't write it off! You won't need to organize transportation from the Mass, you can decorate freely to create whatever atmosphere you like, and tables and chairs will most likely be provided free of charge;

- Hotels;

- Golf courses;

- Vineyards;

- Restaurants with a banquet area;

- Farms or barns with event spaces.

Reception Elements

Some venues offer reception packages in which one price includes the entire shindig, such as seating, tables, linens, serving ware, and a wait staff. Packages typically cost more than renting or purchasing items on your own, yet if you have room in your budget and would prefer not having to fill a mostly empty space from scratch, they're a convenient option.

If you decide to go the a la carte route, here's a basic rundown of what you might need to provide:

- *Food and drink*—Think outside the catering company box. My brother and sister-in-law served amazing food from their favorite Italian chain for their reception dinner, for about half the cost of a catered meal. At another wedding I went to, the couple brought in a casual buffet from a local barbecue spot. If you're planning to serve alcohol, check that your venue has a liquor license and consider purchasing beer, wine, and champagne from a wholesale distributor to save a little cash.

❖   *Places to sit and to eat*—Compare prices at event rental companies for linens, serving ware, utensils, chairs, and tables (don't forget spots for cake, gifts, and a bar).

❖   *Decorations*—Consider flowers, centerpieces, signs, and candles or strands of white lights. They can be as simple or as fancy as you want.

Dancing with Dignity (Is the Chicken Dance Ever Dignified?)

Just like the Macarena practically forces you to do the whole hand-hand, head-head, hip-hip-turn thing, and a waltz encourages its namesake dance, a particular song is often best suited to a certain setting and type of dancing. If I can just be frank for a second, skip the club stuff that basically encourages sex on the dance floor. That's not to say pop and Top 40 songs are off limits—they're fun because they're familiar and they just sound good for dancing. I'd encourage you, though, to check that anything super suggestive or outright trashy stays on your "do not play" list and just keep things classy. Our bodies have such dignity. Dancing in a way expressing that dignity, to music that doesn't degrade who we are, is a way to honor it.

Airborne Unmentionables and Other Traditions

I went to one great, formal wedding full of special dances and family speeches, and another great wedding where the bride and groom served beers out of coolers on the porch and had all their guests go up for the buffet at once, rather than calling table numbers. The point is, there's no rulebook saying you have to make your reception a certain way just to follow convention. Generally, if the two of you are feeling at ease and having fun, your guests will, too.

My dad and uncles insist on taking turns spinning each other on the floor, on their backs, when "Y.M.C.A" comes on at any wedding. I don't know if your family traditions are as weird as mine, but regardless, the customs you choose to include in your reception are up to you. Most couples incorporate some combination of a first dance, parent dances, best man and maid of honor toasts, maybe a bouquet and garter toss, and any traditions or cultural observances unique to your family. When deciding which traditions to include, consider what aspects of your day you feel most sentimental about, then think of how certain traditions can help highlight them. For instance, it really mattered to me that my godmother, who has written poems and funny stories for other family events, give a toast, but doing a bouquet toss didn't matter much. Most of my friends were either engaged, married, or in serious relationships at the time, and tossing the flowers would have been to an visibly small crowd. Instead, our DJ suggested an anniversary dance, where my bouquet went as a gift to the longest-married couple. I don't, however, recommend doing the same with the garter.

The garter. Watching a thigh-grab in front of the bride's dad, brother, and the rest of her family and friends can run anywhere from mildly awkward to completely raunchy. It's your choice, of course, whether or not to include a garter toss, but I have to say I've never witnessed one that doesn't, at some point, make at least a few people in the room blush. If it *is* important to you to toss it, I'd encourage you to talk with your DJ beforehand about your expectations, your tolerance for embarrassment and attention, and your view of what's appropriate. But just because you opt not to fling the garter doesn't mean you can't wear one!

An Invitation to Prayer

The sacramental part of your day doesn't end when you walk out of the church. It's customary at Catholic weddings for the priest to lead your guests in prayer and grace before the meal. Proper etiquette, therefore, calls for inviting him to the reception and counting him in for dinner. Depending on your family dynamics, asking your parents to say a blessing or prayer over you can also be meaningful. At one wedding I learned about a Polish tradition wherein the newlyweds are greeted at the reception by their parents, bearing bread sprinkled with salt and wine. The bread is a prayer that their children will never hunger or be needy, the salt that the bride and groom can meet life's tears and struggles with love, and the wine that the couple never thirst for health, happiness, or good friends. At that wedding the parents also presented the couple with a cross for their home. If your parents raised you in the faith strongly enough that you're having a Catholic wedding, then prayer for the two of you—whether at the reception or privately—on your wedding day can be a wonderful gift as you enter into your vocation.

Expressing Gratitude

Your friends and relatives are either booking flights or driving long distances, buying presents and probably new outfits, and embarrassing themselves doing the Electric Slide, all for love of you. So show them the appreciation they deserve. Aside from the obvious matter of thank-you notes for shower and wedding gifts, there's also the seemingly impossible one of getting some face time with each of your guests.

It's tough when your attention is pulled in so many directions, yet with some effort and planning, you really can spend a little time with everyone throughout the day. The traditional receiving line after the ceremony tends to clog up quickly, feels superficial, and interferes with the photographer's needs, delaying everyone's arrival to the reception. If, like most couples, you decide to forego that, the simplest way to visit your guests is to make the rounds at each table during the reception meal. Yes, this probably means you'll have to get your own food boxed up for later (I suggest tanking up on the cocktail-hour items before the wedding party introductions and your big entrance), but this is a major instance of other people taking priority over you and your appetite.

Simply put, anyone who's valuable enough in your lives (or your families' lives) to warrant an invitation also warrants at least a few minutes of your time, in gratitude for their presence. Don't worry; most guests will understand that they aren't the only ones you need and want to talk to. Be present and sincere in your brevity, pose for a quick photo, give hugs, handshakes, and kisses all around, and then move on.

Ultimately, don't forget that at the day's end all thanks goes to the One who gave you to each other and who is Love itself. Praise God, from whom all blessings flow.

A Sample Reception Schedule

You'll only end up stressed if you create a down-to-the-minute timeline of events for the day, but it can be helpful to have a rough schedule for the sake of order. It also simplifies things for your DJ or emcee and makes transitions easier. In other words, it's probably counterproductive to block in exactly twelve minutes for speeches and four for the cake cutting, but it *is* helpful to know the cake-cutting will be sometime during the last hour. That gives you a guideline for including all the traditions you'd like, while still leaving plenty of time for dancing and socializing.

Here's a skeleton reception schedule. This order keeps things moving without much lag time between major events, but of course, you're welcome to move them around:

Reception start time: _____

❖ Cocktails and appetizers for guests

At this point, you and your wedding party will probably still be taking photos and traveling to the reception. About an hour is long enough for you to snap photos and take a breath before you enter the party. Keep in mind that stretching the time between the Mass and reception much longer can seem inconsiderate— your guests are there for you, and they want to see you and celebrate! Talk with your photographer beforehand about building in a few shorter blocks of time when you newlyweds can duck out of the party for photos when your guests are otherwise occupied with dancing or hanging out.

❖ Wedding party entrances

❖ You might want to have your first dance here . . .

❖ Toasts and blessings, including grace

❖ Meal

You two and your wedding party will probably be served first. Eat fast, because after your guests are served is the perfect time to make the rounds, stopping briefly at each table to greet everyone and thank them for coming. See the section on expressing gratitude (p. 74).

❖ ... Or have your first dance here

❖ Open the dance floor

❖ Special dances: father-daughter, mother-son, and any others

❖ Dancing

Once your guests are dancing and chatting by the middle of the reception, it's a good time for the two of you to sneak away for another photo session with your photographer. Again, it's polite to keep it reasonably short so you can spend time with your guests.

❖ Cake cutting

❖ Bouquet and/or garter toss

❖ Last dance and exit

---------------- ❖ *From the Groom* ❖ ----------------

Staying Real in the Spotlight

Whether or not you enjoy the spotlight, it's hard to avoid being in it on your wedding day. My biggest concern was that with all the attention and photos, I wouldn't feel like my real self in front of everyone. I wanted to be fully present for the Mass and to express my love to Stephanie in a way that felt authentic and not like how I "should" act in front of a camera. Despite your best efforts, it can be tough acting the way you normally do when everyone's watching, and awkward to know every kiss might end up on Facebook. We both prayed about this worry beforehand, and during the day itself we tried to focus on each other and on the experiences, especially during events when everyone's cameras come out, like the first dance or the cake-cutting. I asked God for the grace to feel peaceful about all eyes being on us, and for the ability to just enjoy the day with my bride, my family, and my friends without any pressure to act a certain way. To my grateful relief, I barely noticed the photographer and the attention once things were underway.

◈ *For Conversation* ◈

If you're in the process of choosing a reception venue, together list the words you'd like your guests to remember the party by and use it to identify the sort of location you're drawn to. Consider the atmosphere you'd like to create (casual or formal), as well as your needs (i.e., how many guests you'll need to accommodate, and whether you'd like to look for reception packages or pay for services and materials a la carte).

A friend and I once had a long conversation about a paper she had written arguing that, on their wedding day, a bride and groom have a moral responsibility for their guests through the choices the couple makes about such matters as limiting alcohol and selecting music that discourages overly sexual dancing. Do you agree? List some concrete ways to create a reception atmosphere that discourages temptations while still being moderate and fun.

What family, religious, and wedding-related traditions are important to you? Are there any you'd like to start? If you disagree about some traditions, aim to identify the root of your different views and brainstorm ways to meet in the middle.

How do you each feel about spending an entire day in the spotlight? If the thought makes you want to hide from everyone, make a list of concrete ways to pray for feeling at ease and handling the attention gracefully.

Reception
Planning Sheet

Approximate Guest Count: _____

Prospective venue	Pricing	

	Notes *(Likes/dislikes, what you'll need to provide, and other info)*

TO DOs

First Steps

☐ Narrow down reception locations and schedule visits.

☐ Book your reception site.

☐ Exchange numbers and e-mail addresses with your site's point of contact.

☐ Determine the reception items provided by your site and what you'll need to rent or otherwise provide. Factor them into your budget (see Budget Planning Sheet).

Details and Traditions

☐ Choose your first dance song.

_____

☐ Choose songs for your father-daughter and mother-son dances (if you like, you can also combine the parent dances).

_____

_____

☐ Identify members of your family and wedding party whom you'd like to invite to give a speech or toast—give them at least a few months' notice!

_____

_____

☐ Decide which wedding and family traditions you'd like to incorporate into the reception (e.g., special dances, blessings, a bouquet toss, etc.).

_____

_____

_____

_____

_____

_____

As Your Wedding Day Approaches

☐ If your site doesn't have designated areas for things like a buffet, DJ, cake table, gift area, and dance floor, map out where each of them will be positioned in the room. Ask your venue contact person if the site has software that designs/formats the space.

☐ Figure out seating arrangements. I suggest diagramming where the tables will be in the room (now is a good time to number the tables), writing each guest's name on a sticky note and arranging until the seats are filled in a way that you like.

☐ Create contact sheets for your reception point of contact and vendors (a sample sheet follows).

Decide who will take care of post-reception details

Clean-up:

_____

Collecting and transporting gifts and cards:

_____

Returning rented items:

_____

Donating centerpieces and extra food, flowers, and favors, or distributing them among guests:

_____

_____

_____

_____

CONTACT SHEET

Phone Numbers for the

Bride	
Groom	
Best man	
Maid of honor	
Parents of the bride	
Parents of the groom	
Church	
Celebrant	
Sacristan	
Music director	
Reception site point of contact	
Photographer	
DJ	
Florist	
Caterer	
Other	

Chapter Five
Holding On to Your Sanity

So far, we've broken down the technical side of planning your wedding day and the events leading up to it. Although that's of major importance, it's only half the story. Even the first steps of planning can have an emotional side, too. This chapter aims to break down those matters of the heart.

Silencing the Bridezilla Within

Every bride, including me, accidentally unleashes her inner monstress at times. Two pieces of advice helped me come back down to earth. First, "Don't expect perfection on your wedding day," one friend told me, "or you'll only end up disappointed." I had experienced firsthand how stressful it felt to pick from a hundred different choices for flowers and music and food, deal with the strangers who all had an opinion on how we should do things, and keep two families informed about appointments and dates. I was trying and mostly succeeding to be relaxed about the whole process, knowing an absolutely perfect day was impossible. What got my attention about my friend's advice was the disappointment part. It occurred to me that there was a difference between wanting a "perfect" day so things would feel more relaxed, and wanting a perfect day because perfection alone would make me happy. I was convinced that the simple fact of ending the day married to my best friend would make it one of the best days of my life. I didn't want to tear down that happiness with my own elevated expectations.

The second piece of advice that calmed me was to pray for peace. A friend of mine got married about a month before me, and she shared with me how praying Saint Francis of Assisi's prayer, the one that begins, "Make me a channel of your peace," lifted so much heaviness from her heart. Guests who never RSVP'd? Make me a channel of your peace. Photographer bails with just weeks to go? Make me a channel of your peace. The maid of honor arrives late to the rehearsal? You get the idea.

On the morning of my best friend's wedding, her shoes went missing. After wiping her tears and climbing over the contents of her closet, which had been desperately emptied onto the entire floor, she had to accept she wasn't going to find them and still get out the door on time. "I need new shoes, then," she said. "Let's get going." And off we went to help her pick out a pair of silvery ballet flats on the way to the church.

Understandably, any bride would have a meltdown if she suddenly discovered she had nothing to wear on her feet for some of the biggest footsteps she'll ever take. But my friend's eventual presence of mind and restored sense of peace were the exact grace she needed. Grace isn't something we deserve, yet in God's loving mercy, we're granted "*favor, the free and undeserved help* that God gives us."[1] A peaceful heart is the fruit of grace, one that flows from knowing he alone brings rest when you can't seem to quiet your mind from all the items still on your to-do list. Ask the Lord to make you a vessel, open and ready to be filled with the Holy Spirit. Ask him to work in you as a channel of his peace.

It's easy to start thinking you have to make all the phone calls, send all the e-mail reminders, and put together all the favors yourself. Who else could possibly understand your organizing system or remember everything on your endless checklists?

That's a lie. You're never entirely on your own, and that's a good thing.

Your wedding will happen in communion with your guests and the whole Church. There's no reason the months leading up to it should be spent in isolation. Chances are, plenty of family members and friends will ask what they can do to help. Include them, and reduce your own load, by taking them up on their offers: invite your friends over for an invitation stuffing and addressing party, enlist your crafty aunt for favor and centerpiece inspiration, ask the best man or maid of honor to help research flights for your honeymoon. Requesting and receiving help humbles you and frees up room in your heart for deep, abiding peace.

The Art of Compromise

If you'd like a glimpse of me at my shallowest, literally shedding tears over an ice bucket, flip ahead to chapter 8, where my

---

1. *Catechism of the Catholic Church,* for use in the United States of America, copyright © 1997, United States Catholic Conference, Inc.—Libreria Editrice Vaticana, no. 1996.

husband regales you with the story of our wedding registry and the fights that came with it. I knew getting married involved a lot of flexibility and conceding to each other's wants and needs, yet compromise wasn't my first thought when I was lobbying Andrew for a wedding party flash mob and monogrammed shams. Spoiler alert: I didn't get either of them. My life went on just fine.

One of the best ways, we found, to stay loving through the endless decisions came from a bridal magazine. It suggested that each of us list our top three or four wedding day priorities—the items that felt least negotiable—and try to make them happen for each other while worrying less about the rest. Andrew's top three included the Mass readings, photography, and affordable attire for the groomsmen. Mine also included Mass readings, along with reception music and wedding colors. To be honest, it felt contrived to do a relationship exercise from a magazine. Contrived, perhaps, but surprisingly effective. Suddenly we were free from feeling the magnitude of every little choice. We could just relax about big things like menus, all the way down to small things like centerpieces.

Most importantly, compromise was (and still is) a chance to grow in respect. I've been there, obsessively analyzing every blossom for my bouquet and convinced everyone will notice if it's the wrong shade of pink. As easy as it is to laugh at those anxieties in hindsight, I know how pressing they feel in the moment. During our engagement, Andrew and I started to realize each other's emotional states deserved to be met with love, no matter how ludicrous the circumstances that caused them. When I cried two days before our wedding because the instructions for assembling a cupcake tower might as well have been written in Sanskrit, Andrew didn't tell me not to cry, or ask why an overpriced pile of cardboard had made me so upset. "I'm sorry it's so hard for you right now," he said. "Is there anything I can do?"

He didn't invalidate or brush off my feelings. He recognized them. Despite knowing this was a moment of complete madness on my part, he made me feel understood. That sort of respect and attention to how the other is feeling isn't valuable only during your wedding week. It's an essential part of lasting love, one you can start practicing now.

Money, Your Frenemy

Chapter Two encouraged candor and charity in all things as you prepare for married life. In my experience, money was the topic least likely to encourage the charity part. Most likely, each half of a couple has a slightly different (if not vastly different) approach to finances. Shelling out for wedding expenses we didn't initially anticipate, like a fee to the church and tips for vendors, added up unbelievably fast. The array of options available for practically every detail brought out the spender in me and the saver in Andrew.

You don't have to live together to test-run married life (more on why not in Chapter Seven). Learning and respecting one another's spending patterns now, I'd argue, is actually an even better way to prepare for life together. During yet another late-night, long-distance conversation in which Andrew asked if I really needed the Pad Thai and nail polish I casually mentioned I'd just bought, something occurred to me: in a matter of months my shopping habit wouldn't only belong to me anymore. It would be *our* money, not just mine, that I was forking over a little too readily. Sounds obvious, but honestly, I was shortsighted about my spending for ages. Looking ahead to our wedding also made other parts of our future feel more real and not as distant as they'd used to: a house, babies, vacations. . . . With these future expenses, all very worthy, in mind, I suddenly had new, concrete reasons to build a habit of saying no to nonessential purchases.

It's the rare couple who doesn't stress about their financial life while planning the most expensive day of their lives. Mindfulness about money doesn't mean you keep each other on a leash or analyze your spouse-to-be's every purchase. Your approach to money, however (among other things, like sex and disagreements), can be a very telling barometer of your relationship as a whole: Is it honest? Flexible? Does your approach encourage discussion or shut it down? Practicing solid communication and moderation in your pre- and post-wedding spending will amplify your ability to live out these virtues in all other areas of your life together, too.

Speaking of moderation, I've heard stories of couples going thousands of dollars into debt to finance the wedding of their dreams. Can I be blunt here? Don't do it. Yes, it would be nice to have a diamond eternity band, designer gown, or all-inclusive Caribbean honeymoon. But if those things aren't in the cards for your financial situation, I truly hope you would be just as happy getting married in an inexpensive secondhand dress and not going on a honeymoon at all. It's your spouse, not your stuff, that makes a marriage.

Let Nothing Disturb You

The world is a noisy place. Like most of us, I usually fill silences with sound. I constantly catch myself missing opportunities to retreat from the noise. I play music most days on my way to work, but when I'm in the car with Andrew, he prefers to leave the radio off so we can talk or pray the Rosary. Sometimes it makes me impatient, but I see more and more how wise he is—ditching the noise almost always leads to some of our best conversations and teaches me to be more present.

Engagement is noisy as well, with all its meetings, solicited and unsolicited advice, and increased communication with family and friends. Take time to renew your soul in the quiet, in silence. You'll find Jesus there. In silence the Holy Spirit came upon Mary in her room in Nazareth, in silence Jesus grew in her womb, and in silence our salvation was so humbly born, alone with his parents in a dirty old barn.

So here are my suggestions for tuning out the noise and entering into silence:

- ❖ Kneel before the Lord together. Take your fiancé on a prayer date, whether to Eucharistic adoration or even to an empty chapel, and revel in Christ's presence. Leaving the church afterward feels like reentering the world.

- ❖ Quiet your bridal brain for a night: go out to dinner, or cook it yourself, and forbid yourselves to talk about anything wedding-related. After a rough day of going crazy with the registry scanner, the lady who helped us at the department store advised us to do just that. It was exactly what Andrew and I needed to regain a perspective on what wedding matters weren't important and to remember we still had plenty of time to complete what felt like endless obligations.

- ❖ Spend an evening unplugged. Turn off your computers, your phones, and your music, and soak in everything else the world has to offer. Stargazing with blankets and cocoa? A long walk where you can wander somewhere you've never gone? Dessert and board games by candlelight? Yes.

◈ Go for a run, a hike, a bike ride . . . exercise is such a good way to burn off your stress, and gives you the option of talking or just reflecting while you're together.

◈ Write to each other. Putting your heart on paper in your best handwriting is an exercise in concentration, and background music or lit-up screens don't make it any easier. To me, hardly anything is more special than a handwritten note where your love's words don't come with a backspace key.

Ultimately, when in doubt, trust where you feel peace. Follow your peace. Decisions that bring you unrest are probably worth reconsidering. I'll leave you with the words of Saint Teresa of Avila, one of my favorite prayers:

> Let nothing disturb you,
> Let nothing frighten you,
> All things are passing away:
> God never changes.
> Patience obtains all things
> Whoever has God lacks nothing;
> God alone suffices.

────────────── ◈ *From the Groom* ◈ ──────────────

Cultivating Peace Even When You Feel Too Busy

Steph's suggestions about creating peace, especially frequent adoration, date nights, and limiting your technology use when you're together, don't apply only to pre-wedding madness. Engagement can be a heightened time of busyness, but life is always busy in some way. I've heard it said that it's often when you're busiest and think you don't even have time to pray or go to Mass that you need it most. Give your time to God and he will multiply it and give you every grace you need to get through whatever you're stressed about.

◈ *For Conversation* ◈

Identify possible origins of the culture's insistence that bachelor/bachelorette parties have an anything goes, all-bets-are-off mentality. What are the effects of this mindset on engaged couples?

What is your biggest source of stress as you navigate your wedding planning process? Identify specific ways to combat it and let the small stuff go.

Robin Williams' character reminds Matt Damon's character, Will Hunting, in the film *Good Will Hunting,* that Will isn't perfect, and neither is the woman he loves. Love, Williams says, isn't about perfection, but about whether two people are perfect for each other. Have your approaches to compromise and patience changed as you've gone from dating to engagement? Discuss changes for the better and for the worse, and talk about ways to foster love and understanding as you plan your wedding.

Try the planning exercise my husband and I did as we hashed out our budget and personal preferences: using the Budget Worksheet, list each of your top three wedding priorities and shape your decisions accordingly.

Discuss your individual habits when it comes to spending. Come up with a few ways to deal with your different tendencies and to spend moderately.

Chapter Six
Beauty and the Bride

The Pressure to Be Beautiful

BRIDES, THIS CHAPTER is written to you. It goes without saying that as women, we receive hundreds of messages every single day about how we're supposed to look. We need to wear this to look attractive to a guy, say that to make him want us, put on makeup to cover every flaw.

For most of my teenage and young adult years, I was blessed with few self-image struggles. When I got engaged and started looking at bridal magazines and websites, though, I'd suddenly start wishing I could be a little skinnier, clear up my skin, whiten my teeth. I *knew* it was all unnecessary and those messages were total lies, but the pressure to be beautiful suddenly felt impossible to ignore. For brides-to-be, all the normal pressures feel a hundred times more intense. It's fine to want to look pretty, of course, but at a time when all eyes would soon be on me for an entire day, I found it didn't take much to make me too hard on myself.

But beauty isn't something we put on in the morning; it's something we *already possess*. Can you imagine what it would be like if the fashion industry realized this? Femininity is anything but a selling point; it's nothing less than who we are.

Beautiful Because We Are

When I say femininity is *who we are*, I'm speaking literally: "male and female he created them" (Gen 1:27) Our creation in God's image goes straight to the Garden, where the first man and woman were able to rejoice completely and purely in one another, body and soul. Love, nakedness, and even desire were present, but not lust, at least before sin entered the picture.

One of the culture's biggest lies is that romance, beauty, and sexiness are only possible when a woman inspires lust in a man (by the way, lust is *not* the same as passion or desire; those things are goods that can be freely given out of love for the other, while lust seeks to take and to satisfy only the self). We're told we'll never be good enough, never be pretty enough. But this couldn't be further from the truth. It took a lot of reorienting for my heart to finally realize it. Deep down, every woman (and every man) knows it: she is so much more than just a body; so much more than her looks.

God's love for every human person is written right into our bodies and into how we're created. What that means for you, as a bride and as a daughter of God, is that your body is profoundly good. We, as human persons, possess immense dignity and worth simply because we exist, created out of love by Love. Authentic beauty is an inherent part of who women are created to be—it's the cry of our hearts. No amount of makeup or working out can alter it or improve it, because it's already there.

The Genius of Women

I felt myself being purified, broken, and remade dozens of times during my engagement. I wanted so badly to stop leaving my towels on the floor, to spend more time in prayer, to actually get up when my alarm went off, and, most of all, to overcome all the sins I kept falling into, all before I got married. In my mind, everything needed to be improved upon and perfected before I was worthy of becoming Andrew's wife.

Ultimately, being reminded of my dignity, beauty, and particular gifts as a woman was one of the best ways to prepare myself, in whatever humble way I could, to become a wife and, eventually, a mother. In college, I was introduced to *Mulieris Dignitatem*, Saint John Paul II's letter on the dignity of women, but had never read it. When I finally cracked it open before my wedding, I was blown away. The Pope writes so eloquently about the gifts that women alone, with Mary as their model, can offer their husbands, families, and the Church.

The media tends to present the Church as looking down on women, limiting their freedom and seeing them as secondary to men. In reality, that couldn't be further from the truth. Woman, after all, is the very last being that God creates, and Adam's reaction is filled with awe: "This at last is bone of my bones and flesh of my flesh!" (Gen 2:23). Make no mistake: women are the crown of creation. In his letter, John Paul II goes so far as to say that women have a unique "genius" in how they live, serve, love, and worship.

"The Church gives thanks," he says, *"for all the manifestations of the feminine 'genius'* which have appeared in the course of history . . . she gives thanks for all *the fruits of feminine holiness."*[1]

The Song of Songs: A Marriage Made in Heaven

When I was fifteen, I heard a song that completely changed the way I look at love, marriage, and Scripture. My church youth group hopped on a bus and drove an hour for a performance by Matt Maher, a Catholic musician. At the time, I was atrociously shy, so I wasn't very much into the youth group, and I also wasn't much into Christian music. To my surprise, I began to enjoy the show, and by the time Matt introduced a song called "Set Me as a Seal," I was all in.

This song, he said, was his take on the greatest love song ever written. The Song of Songs lies in the middle of the Bible—a marriage situated between the first marriage of Adam and Eve in Genesis at the beginning, and the heavenly wedding feast in Revelation at the end. It's a dialogue in poetry between two lovers as they search for each other and, ultimately, rejoice in the love they find in one another.

Two soul mates searching and searching, then finally finding each other? My romantic, barely-had-a-boyfriend high school self was caught up in every word. Matt's song was beautiful, and as soon as I got home I opened my Bible to read the original. I was floored. A sampling:

> As an apple tree among the trees of the wood,
> so is my beloved among young men.

---

1. John Paul II, *Mulieris Dignitatem* (Boston: Pauline Books & Media, 2013), IX.31.

With great delight I sat in his shadow,
    and his fruit was sweet to my taste.
He brought me to the banqueting house,
    and his intention toward me was love.
Sustain me with raisins,
    refresh me with apples;
      for I am faint with love.
O that his left hand were under my head,
    and that his right hand embraced me! (Song 2:3–6)

Until then, I'd had no idea Scripture could be sexy. The ache, the longing for love, rang so true. What's more, I realized for the first time that sex and love can say the same thing: I revere, I desire, I adore you, and I will do battle with evil and with death itself for you to know my love.

Seeing for Real

I was struck as well by the lover's wonderment at his bride's perfection. When you consider that the Song of Songs echoes Christ's deep, self-emptying love for his bride, the Church, in the language of earthly marriage, it not only makes a lot of sense; it's an incredible picture of a man reveling in the feminine beauty of his beloved:

You have ravished my heart, my sister, my bride,
    you have ravished my heart with a glance of your eyes,
    with one jewel of your necklace.
How sweet is your love, my sister, my bride!
    how much better is your love than wine,
    and the fragrance of your oils than any spice!
Your lips distil nectar, my bride;
    honey and milk are under your tongue;
    the scent of your garments is like the scent of Lebanon.

> A garden locked is my sister, my bride,
>   a garden locked, a fountain sealed. (Song 4:9–12)

In full disclosure, the woman's hair also gets compared to a flock of goats and her neck to a tower outfitted for battle, which probably wouldn't turn on many women these days. But the bridegroom's sense of wonder still rings true. These lovers truly see each other.

In the movie *Avatar* characters greet one another with "I see you" instead of "hello." This expression of seeing another person resonated deep within me—it's so much more than using your eyes to look at another; it's taking in a deeper vision of the person that he or she is. That's how the lovers in the Song of Songs *see*—their attraction isn't just to the other's physical appearance. It is a pull toward the other person in his or her entirety.

Receiving Beauty Is Receiving Love

"You have ravished my heart." Not just your body or your face, but *you*. Body and soul can't be separated, and together they form a full, beautifully authentic expression of love. I hope the man you're marrying sees you exactly like that: purely, passionately, and amazed at everything you are.

You know those days when you haven't showered, put on makeup, or maybe even changed out of your sweats? If a man has ever called you beautiful in such a state, and if you've ever brushed it off, telling him there's no way you look beautiful with your unwashed hair or your breakouts or your frump gear, I'm calling it out. Believe me, I've been there, too. But it's time we, as women, trust the men we love and their compliments.

Most times when I'm complaining about my appearance, it's not that I just want to hear my husband tell me nice things about myself. It's that I truly don't feel pretty. Something about how we're created links beauty and worth so closely in a woman's heart. If I dig deeper when I'm struggling with my looks, it usually comes down to desiring to hear that I am lovable.

When I'm repeatedly falling into certain sins or haven't been to Confession in a while, I'm harder on myself when it comes to beauty. I think of appearance as an easily visible, external measure of feeling good about oneself. When we're feeling bad about who we are on the inside, it's easy to blame some other aspect of ourselves that lies on the outside—when I feel like my soul is ugly, *I* feel ugly, which manifests itself in disliking how I look. By contrast, when I feel peace about how I *am*, praying often and trying to practice sacrificial love, I also feel a greater peace about how I look.

Let me be clear: caring about how we look isn't wrong in itself. But vanity and insecurity are traps. They can indicate a deeper, more internal struggle with feeling worthy. When you're down on yourself, ask God for the grace to see yourself as he sees you. Hard as it might be to believe, he sees nothing less than a beautiful daughter made in his image. Ask him for freedom from insecurity, freedom from anxiety about your looks. Seek his mercy in prayer and in the confessional, and watch as a newfound inner contentment brings richer contentment in every part of your life.

Over time, my husband has opened my eyes to the idea that receiving compliments from him is a major way of receiving his love. If I reject his words, it feels like I'm rejecting *him*. Moreover, it hurt him, he said, to see me so unaware and unbelieving of my beauty. I was so stunned the first time he told me that—amid all my complaints, I certainly hadn't meant to throw Andrew's gestures of love back in his face. I want to encourage us as women, myself included, to take good men at their word—it's a gift when someone recognizes beauty within us. Our dignity is so great that acknowledging it with grace is the only fitting response.

Choosing Your Dress

So, what does this idea of authentic beauty mean when it comes to how you look on your wedding day? Saying "yes" to the dress is no small task, obviously. As a Catholic bride, there's the added consideration of modesty—bear in mind that some churches have guidelines about the bride's attire, and that your marriage is meant to be an earthly witness to divine love for all who attend. Before you dismiss modesty as something repressive where, you know, muumuus are the only acceptable clothing, consider what it really means.

Since we're made in the very image of God, who is goodness, truth, and beauty, how could our bodies be anything but? Modesty is covering the body not because it's bad or shameful but because it's so good, so precious, that it's not meant for just anyone or anything. A bride doesn't wear a veil to hide but to reserve the first real look at her face for her bridegroom alone.

I'd encourage you to think of your wedding dress in the same sense—there are plenty of pre-wedding arm and butt workouts and gowns designed to show off every curve, yet when you're about to give all of yourself, body and soul, to one person forever, doesn't it make sense to dress in a way that reflects it? True, others might admire your body in a tight or low-cut dress, but you're too good, too beautiful to be put on display, and you shouldn't be wearing the dress for others anyway. So consider modesty an invitation: an invitation to be looked at with love, not lust; an invitation to reveal God's love through your beauty; an invitation to be seen as so much more than just a body.

When it comes to picking out your wedding dress (and your bridesmaids' dresses), a good practical approach is to choose a dress that covers your breasts, back, and bottom in a way that's not skintight and that takes your body type into account. If you're smaller-chested, for instance, a strapless dress might offer plenty of coverage, but a larger-busted bride might require straps and a higher neckline. That certainly doesn't mean you should choose something unflattering. If virtue is the moderate choice between two extremes, consider beauty the virtue that lies between underplaying your beauty and revealing too much of it. Our bodies and our beauty aren't meant to be diminished but accentuated in a way that speaks to our inner worth.

It also doesn't mean modesty is just a set of rules. Rules exist to cultivate true freedom, not to suppress it. In the past I sometimes wore outfits that fit too tightly or dipped too low and could barely concentrate on what I was doing because I was constantly yanking at my clothes. But when my clothes fit properly and have more coverage, I feel so much more at ease. That's when I feel free—free from everything from wandering bra straps to hems that ride up to anxiety about who is seeing what. It adds up to freedom from being objectified.

Saint John Paul II said that Christ "assigns the dignity of every woman as a task to every man."[2] Incredible, right? Every human person possesses tremendous dignity simply because he or she *is*. We women possess it in a special way—through our beauty. Sadly, it's easy to see the ways beauty has been twisted by the culture, in both men's and women's eyes. But we can get it back when we

---

2. Saint John Paul II, *Man and Woman He Created Them: A Theology of the Body* (Boston: Pauline Books & Media, 2006), 519.

know and understand who we are before God. The dignity of both you and your husband-to-be merits only one response: pure love, free from lust or selfishness. As long as we're on earth, we won't be perfect at dignity, but we can invite it in the best way we can.

By the way, don't feel relegated only to bridal shops, especially for your bridesmaids. It's easily possible to find pretty, festive dresses, usually at lower price points, from department stores and chain retailers at the mall and from online boutiques. And if you don't mind a bit of variety, you can even ask your maids to choose their own dresses in your wedding colors. One bride I know simply asked her bridesmaids to wear a black cocktail dress, and the result was elegant and chic. As for your wedding gown, online auctions feature once-worn or never-worn dresses, sometimes from major designers for less than their original retail price, and vintage stores can offer hip, romantic choices. If you'd like to add your own vintage twist, a bit of lace, beading, or trim from your mom's or grandmother's wedding dress added to your own is special and sweet.

A Loving Gaze

After my first baby was born—with me still looking six months' pregnant, sleeping very little, and showering even less, plus all the demands of caring for a newborn—my relationship with Andrew felt secondary. It was only a temporary necessity, but still we hardly had any time for romance or intimacy. That lack of time for one another showed itself in more frequent arguments, with more of our weaknesses on display than ever before.

A few months later, among our many attempts to be good to one another and meet these demands with love, Andrew told me about a strategy he had come up with for loving me better. He said that for a couple weeks he had made a conscious effort to spend a few minutes a day just looking at me—not staring dreamily into my eyes, but only watching as I went about my business. That simple gaze, he said, was so powerful in making him present and still during those stressful days, and in calling to mind all the reasons he loved me.

I was floored. Each of us wants so desperately to be seen. It's not narcissism or begging for attention; it's a deep desire of our hearts. I frequently remember the words of a man I met on the streets of Philadelphia. He said the hardest thing about being homeless and poor wasn't that only a few people gave him money or stopped to talk; it was that so many walked by him without so much as a glance, as if not looking meant they didn't have to think about him even for a second. My heart stirred, and having formerly been one to walk by most of the time, I resolved then to start making eye contact and saying hello to people I encountered who probably don't get looked at often enough. Being looked at taps into something essential: it says you are dignified, you are deserving of respect and attention, you are worthy.

If a simple look has that profound an effect on someone we're just walking by on the street, imagine the power a look can have when it's from your spouse, amplified with love and a shared history. Even during a time when my self-worth was at an all-time low, knowing my husband was taking time out of his day to do nothing but gaze upon me, his bride, felt immensely loving. As soon as Andrew told me about it, I realized that in the busyness of being new parents, entire days had passed where we never really spent time just absorbing one another's presence. I decided to follow suit, and can personally attest to the intimacy and affection a look can generate. In those moments, annoyances seem less annoying and frustrations that felt huge suddenly don't seem so big. They don't go away, but time spent looking at one another seems to fortify us. Believe it or not, that one practice of gazing upon each other forces us to rest in each other, no matter how stressed we are.

Practical Points

Practically speaking, then, what does all this theological talk have to do with the pressure to be beautiful? The truth about authentic, countercultural beauty was a huge consolation to me during times when I struggled with the impossible ideal, the idol really, of bridal perfection. Let it console you, too! Thank God for the gift of your femininity and ask him for the grace to help you see your beauty when you're tempted to reject it. I also suggest:

- Taking frequent, periodic breaks from any website full of wedding images. The strong temptation to compare yourself to other women gets even stronger when you're bombarded with endless resources for bridal fitness, bridal photo checklists, bridal hairdos, and bridal everything else. The easiest way to avoid comparison syndrome is to get rid of the influences that make us most likely to compare.

- Opening your Bible to the Song of Songs—hopefully the passages quoted earlier sparked something in your heart. The bridegroom does nothing but rejoice and revel in his bride's perfection: "you are altogether beautiful, my love; there is no flaw in you" (Song 4:7).

- Prioritizing your physical and emotional well-being. When I make reasonable efforts to eat well, dress nicely, do my hair, or put on a little makeup, I really do feel better about my appearance. Although appearance is on the exterior, the sense of contentment that flows from self-confidence can run much deeper, reminding you of your interior worth.

◈ Looking to Our Lady. Unlike the rest of us, Mary was conceived without sin. After Jesus, she was the most perfect human being to ever walk this earth. In her perfection, Mary reflected all the Lord's qualities in her very life: perfect love, perfect humility, and perfect beauty, inside and out. I began developing a prayer relationship with her in college, and at first I wondered how I'd ever measure up, but friends told me to keep praying to her anyway. I'm grateful I did. In time, I came to see her not as an unattainable ideal but as a loving mother and sister whose qualities I could aspire to. Ask her to reveal to you your beauty and to bear it with grace. I promise she won't leave you wanting.

Pope Benedict XVI wrote:

Too often, though, the beauty that is thrust upon us is illusory and deceitful, superficial and blinding, leaving the onlooker dazed; instead of bringing him out of himself and opening him up to horizons of true freedom as it draws him aloft; it imprisons him within himself and further enslaves him, depriving him of hope and joy. . . . Authentic beauty, however, unlocks the yearning of the human heart, the profound desire to know, to love, to go toward the Other, to reach for the Beyond. If we acknowledge that beauty touches us intimately, that it wounds us, that it opens our eyes, then we rediscover the joy of seeing, of being able to grasp the profound meaning of our existence.[3]

---

3. Pope Benedict XVI, Meeting with Artists at the Sistine Chapel, Nov. 21, 2009. http://w2.vatican.va/content/benedict-xvi/en/speeches/2009/november /documents/hf_ben-xvi_spe_20091121_artisti.html.

You are beautiful, you are enough, and you are loved. Your beauty has the power to reveal truth and goodness and to inspire pure love. Know this, and believe it.

❖ From the Groom ❖

Worthy of Beauty

Even though I'm a man, this chapter resonates deeply with me. So I'd like to offer a few extra words here. When I first noticed Stephanie in my senior-year English class, she captivated me. From her leopard-print shoes (*Do people under 65 wear leopard print? unfashionable Andrew wondered*), to her cleverness and intelligence to her very open and very beautiful smile, what began as curiosity (*What sort of person wears leopard-print shoes? Perhaps I can try to find out . . .*) developed into a full-fledged crush. But it was a crush I was unwilling to admit to anyone—especially myself. I once told a friend, in earnest, "I don't want to date Stephanie, but I hope I can find someone *like* her. I mean, with the same qualities and stuff. Just not *her*."

And yet, despite my insistent non-crush on Stephanie, I'd find myself thinking about her during the day, often after I'd done something less than virtuous. What made me decide to cut back on my cussing? Was I really doing it for a girl I didn't even want to date? What made me start rethinking the seriousness of physical intimacy? The adorable and sharp girl from English class?

What I didn't realize is that I felt the pull of beauty in my heart, a pull that calls those who see beauty to desire becoming worthy of it. After an encounter with the goodness and the beauty that were so undeniably apparent in Stephanie, I was all the more aware of my own unworthiness. (Stephanie later said she had the same worries.) It's a stereotype that some people feel their beloved is out of their league, but there is a nod toward truth in that hackneyed phrase. If God is perfect goodness, truth, and beauty, then an earthly encounter with those qualities had better be transformative. Here was a girl who was so evidently good, so captivatingly beautiful, that I couldn't help but see my own shortcomings when seeing her or thinking about her.

My desire toward worthiness, my aim to improve myself through small acts of self-denial and virtue, came from recognizing, in the face of beauty, what beauty requires of us. In the same way that we could never deserve the ineffable gift of the Eucharist but we still have to strive to be deserving of it, I could never be fully worthy of Stephanie's love, but I could try to live up to the standard she deserved—and still deserves. Beauty, the sort of beauty that serves as a reflection of heaven, is both powerful and transformative.

For Conversation

Is there a beauty-related area of wedding prep that's been a particular struggle for you (e.g., weight, comparison, looks)? Identify a few quotes or Scripture passages you can turn to for reflection when you struggle.

Sometimes it's said that women dress, make themselves up, and do their hair for other women, not for men. Do you agree? If you think this is true, what might be the reason behind it? Talk about pros and cons to this attitude.

Songs like Bruno Mars' "Just the Way You Are" and One Direction's "What Makes You Beautiful" tend to make every woman swoon, or at least say "Aww." What about lyrics like theirs is so universally appealing?

Read the Song of Songs together, alternating the voices of the bride and bridegroom (most Bibles mark the narrator of each section). Discuss passages that stand out to you. How do these verses speak to both earthly marriage and the love between Jesus and the Church?

As I mentioned earlier, that desiring to be beautiful, for me, usually boils down to a desire to be loved. Do you agree? What do you see as the root of a woman's longing to look and feel beautiful?

Chapter Seven
Love Incarnate, A.K.A. the Sex Chapter

The Ache

BE HONEST. Did you skip ahead to this section? I'm right there with you. Why does sex have such a hold over us? Sex is one of life's most profound mysteries. At least in part, its allure has a lot to do with our longing for something infinite, something enduring, and something beyond ourselves.

We spend our lives aching for love, for completion. We thirst. That cry resides deep within us, but it's also made manifest on the outside—in our bodies. Ponder the fact that "a man's body makes no sense by itself; a woman's body makes no sense by itself. Seen in light of each other, the picture becomes complete: we go together . . . Consider the possibility that human sexuality—our maleness and femaleness and the call to 'completion' inherent there—is itself a message from God."[1] How we're created, male and female, is no coincidence. We're made for union.

When you find the one your soul loves, which you have done if you're preparing for marriage, a part of that ache is lessened, but we're still left wanting. It's not your future spouse's fault; it's simply that, whether we recognize it or not, nothing and no one on this earth can ultimately satisfy. "Our hearts are restless, O Lord," wrote Saint Augustine, "until they rest in you." It's the Lord we're really seeking whenever we feel desire, whenever we're moved by beauty, and whenever we get the sense that life holds something more than what we can see and observe.

Free, Faithful, Total, and Fruitful: Theology of the Body (and What It Has to Do with Your Body)

Pope Saint John Paul II spent five years early in his papacy delivering a series of talks on human personhood, sexuality, and spirituality at his weekly audiences. Known as the theology of the body, the Pope's catechesis discusses human existence in light of our creation as man and woman, and our deep longing for union. John Paul II explores the way that marriage, both earthly and divine, images our identity as male and female in light of our ultimate satisfaction: complete and total union with God for all eternity.

Scandalous? A *Pope*? Talking about *sex*? It only seems like it. But radical? Definitely. John Paul II's vision of love upended all of my previous notions about sex—and for the better. He writes:

---

1. Christopher West, *Fill These Hearts* (New York: Random House, 2012), 8.

"Marriage corresponds to the vocation of Christians only when it mirrors the love that Christ, the Bridegroom, gives to the Church, his Bride, and which the Church . . . seeks to give back to Christ in return. This is the redeeming, saving love, the love with which man has been loved by God from eternity in Christ."[2]

Okay. What does all that mean? Essentially, the Pope is identifying Jesus' complete self-gift on the Cross as the ultimate act of love, one that married couples are called to imitate. The concept of love as salvation he refers to is quite literal—a husband and wife are meant to be each other's path to heaven. To get there, love has to be more than a feeling, more than convenience, and more than romance alone. It has to be freely, faithfully, totally, and fruitfully given.

Love is *free* when each spouse willingly chooses the good of the other. Choosing to do whatever you want doesn't make you free. That's just mere license, and you can easily become a slave to your desires. Freedom, on the other hand, is wanting what is good and choosing that good. Making the choice, over and over, to die to yourself by putting your husband or wife first sets you free to love wholeheartedly.

Love that's *faithful* means more than not cheating on your spouse. It means following through on your commitments—commitments as all-encompassing as your wedding vows, and as simple as doing the dishes or filling up the gas tank when you say you will.

Love is *total* when it's given entirely, reserving nothing. Forget the presents for a second; the most real, meaningful, gift you can give your spouse for your wedding is nothing more or less than

---

2. *Man and Woman He Created Them*, 476.

your self. John Paul II often quoted Vatican II: "man . . . cannot fully find himself except through a sincere gift of himself.[3] What does he mean?

The sacraments of the Church make the invisible visible through mediums we can sense and observe, like the water of Baptism and the bread and wine that become the Eucharist. In marriage, the invisible—the mystery of the love of God the Father, Son, and Holy Spirit—is made visible through the body. That is, every time a husband and wife make love, they are expressing with their bodies the words they expressed in their vows on their wedding day. God is pure, sacrificial love. Our call to love like God is inscribed into our very bodies, in our creation as male and female. The body, then, is sacramental. And, like Christ is God's love made flesh, sex is marital love (in which spouses are called to love like God loves) made flesh. It's love made incarnate. Total love means total self-gift.[4]

And lastly, love is meant to be *fruitful*, to bring forth life. Jesus' crucifixion, the most profound act of love, ends not in death but in eternal life. In the same way, married love is meant to be abundant, whether through children, through ministry to the Church, or in other ways.

Why the Catholic Church Wants You to Have the Best Sex

Is all this sounding a little out there? The culture tends to understand sex and God as two entirely different spheres and to

---

3. Vatican II, Pastoral Constitution on the Church in the Modern World, *Gaudium et Spes,* (Boston: Pauline Books & Media, 1966), 24.

4. See Christopher West, *Theology of the Body for Beginners* (West Chester, PA: Ascension Press, 2009).

present the Church as repressive and down on sex. This has led to the pervading idea that one can't be both a religious and a sexual being. In reality, this puritanical approach couldn't be further from the truth.

Back in the Garden of Eden, when God created the first man and woman, he instructed them to "be fruitful and multiply" (Gen 1:28). What he was saying is enjoy your union! Enjoy one another and let it deepen your love. Be married. Be free. May your love be life-giving.

God is love. God created the man and woman for one another, to find in each other the fulfillment of their longing and for their marital union to image God's perfect love. He *wants* married couples to have joyful, body-and-soul-satisfying sexual relationships.

What does that mean? Despite the common perception, it doesn't mean a long list of sexual dos and don'ts, nor a series of rules that reduce sex to a merely functional and necessary act. It doesn't mean the body is bad or desire is shameful.

It means we're meant for freedom. In all things, the Church comes from a place of loving wisdom that intends our fullest happiness, even on tough issues like birth control, pornography, and saving sex for marriage. Saint Paul writes: "For what the flesh desires is opposed to the Spirit, and what the Spirit desires is opposed to the flesh; for these are opposed to each other, to prevent you from doing what you want. But if you are led by the Spirit, you are not subject to the law" (Gal 5:17–18). Saint Paul is saying that guidelines for sexual integrity exist not to burden us but to let us live in the most fulfilling way. There's a reason why you stop at a red light, for instance, or why your phone manual tells you not to take your phone swimming. Arleen Spenceley, a Tampa Bay journalist whose article "Why I'm Still a Virgin at Age 26" went viral in 2012, explains that living out our sexuality with integrity is something that flows from what is naturally good for us. She says chastity can be hard "because it has rubrics in a culture that doesn't like rules. But chastity isn't restrictive like shackles are restrictive. It's restrictive like boundaries: it doesn't hold us back but keeps what is hurtful, unhealthy, or unnecessary out of the way. We are most free when we have healthy boundaries, not when we have none."[5]

In the same way, the Church's teachings on sex aren't meant as a burden. They're intended as a path to true freedom, with the goal being a body, soul, and mind so integrated that the guidelines aren't necessary anymore because we're already living out our sexuality as we were meant to. How can we point ourselves in that direction? Chastity is a roadmap to getting there.

Chastity

Chastity gets a bad rap. Say the word, and what comes to mind is probably something along the lines of the whole *Mean Girls*, don't-have-sex-or-you'll-get-pregnant-and-die approach. If that sounds ridiculous to you, I agree completely. Instead, I invite you to see chastity with fresh eyes and a hopeful, open heart.

In short, chastity is sexual self-control. It's purity in your thoughts, words, and actions, and saving sexually intimate acts for marriage. Over time, I've become convinced firsthand that chastity is one of the surest paths to authentic love and a fulfilling life for anyone, no matter what you've done in the past or whether or not you're a virgin. There's a better case to be made than awkward

---

5. Arleen Spenceley, *Chastity Is for Lovers: Single, Happy, and (Still) a Virgin* (Notre Dame, IN: Ave Maria Press, 2014), 9.

sex-ed scare tactics, one that appeals not just to religion or morals but to the heart.

If it's true that every finite pursuit on this earth, sex included, is the pursuit of the infinite, how are we supposed to deal with it this side of heaven? Chastity enables us to aim our longing in the most fulfilling earthly direction. So, with this in mind, I present a practical, reason-based case for chastity:

> ❖ *It safeguards the future of your relationship.* Studies show that couples who sleep together before marriage have higher rates of divorce and marital infidelity.[6] Those who live together beforehand risk a "cohabitation effect"[7] of staying in unfulfilling relationships longer than they would otherwise, and are statistically more likely to divorce than couples who did not cohabitate.[8] (Note: if you are living together, this doesn't mean your relationship is doomed. And yet, bear in mind that before consenting to officiate your wedding, most parishes require that you live apart for at least six months beforehand. Yes, it will be hard and probably inconvenient, but it will purify your love, train you in sacrifice, and strengthen your marriage before it even starts.) Of course, lots of elements factor

---

6. See Glen T. Stanton, "Premarital Sex and Greater Risk of Divorce." *Focusonthefamily.com.* Focus on the Family, April 2011. http://www.focusonthefamily.com/about_us/focus-findings/marriage/premarital-sex-and-divorce.aspx.

7. See Jay, "The Downside of Cohabitating Before Marriage."

8. See Casey E. Copen, et al. "First Marriages in the United States: Data from the 2006–2010 National Survey of Family Growth." *National Health Statistics Reports* 49 (March 2012): 1-21. http://www.cdc.gov/nchs/data/nhsr/nhsr049.pdf.

into why relationships sometimes end. But if you're serious about the person you love, why not give yourselves the best possible fighting chance? Everyone wants to find love. No one hopes his or her love will end in a breakup or divorce.

◈ *Chastity makes sense within the natural order of things.* Almost anyone can recognize that a natural order exists, and so natural outcomes follow. If we go against that order, natural consequences result—no matter how much I want to fly, for example, I'll still fall from the sky every time. Taking sex out of the natural order has its consequences, too: before contraception was legalized in 1958, there were three known sexually transmitted infections (STIs). Today, about five decades after contraceptives and the sexual revolution lessened the perceived consequences of sex outside of marriage, there are over twenty-five.[9]

◈ *Chastity lets you love with your eyes wide open.* Studies show that oxytocin, the body's bonding hormone, is released in greatest quantities during and after sex and other intimate acts. It tends to make men and women see their partners more favorably: it aids in the forgiveness of flaws and boosts perceived attractiveness, both of which help the couple to stick together.[10] That's great when

---

9. See Medical Institute for Sexual Health, "How Many STIs Are There and What Are Their Names?" 2012 https://www.medinstitute.org/faqs/how-many-stis-are-there-and-what-are-their-names/.

10. See Luciana Gravotta, "Be Mine Forever: Oxytocin May Help Build Long-Lasting Love," *Scientific American*, 2014. http://www.scientificamerican.com/article/be-mine-forever-oxytocin/.

you've entered into a lifelong sexual bond in marriage, but not so great beforehand when you might overlook problems in a relationship. Without the blinders sex can introduce, you can see your relationship, and the person you're dating, for what they are. Should you discern your relationship isn't headed toward forever, it's easier to walk away.

❖ *Chastity makes you free.* Truly. In my opinion, chastity and our identity as sexual beings go far beyond what we're doing (or not doing) in bed. They're about who we are as men and women. True, living out chastity frees you from worries about pregnancy and STIs and can help you end the wrong relationships with fewer regrets. But what's more, I've found chastity enables you to be more content with yourself. It helps you know your standards and sustain your hope, and to be better able to rise above lies the culture tells us about how we should act, look, and date. Living out this virtue can truly contribute to a life more fully, and more freely, lived.

But We're Engaged

If you're already engaged, what's the point of saving sexually intimate acts for marriage? You already know you're only going to be with each other from here on out. But maybe the better question is: What's the point of marriage? Romance, affirmation, and good feelings are pleasant, but they alone aren't love. Love is dying to yourself, choosing time after time to put the good of the other before your own. Marriage means a husband and a wife make the decision to "take up their crosses and so follow him, to rise again after they have fallen, to forgive one another, to bear one another's burdens, to 'be subject to one another out of reverence for Christ,' and to love one another with supernatural, tender, and fruitful love."[11]

That's a tall order. With grace and forgiveness, it's possible. You've probably noticed already that being engaged feels different than just dating. It's a training ground for married life. A surefire path to a good marriage is to practice that kind of loving sacrifice now, including in your physical relationship. Consider a person who can't discipline her sexual desires. What does it mean when this person says "yes" to sex? Nothing. It simply means she can't say "no." But the chaste individual, someone who can and who has said "no" to sexual intimacy before getting married (virgin or not) can truly mean "yes" when the time comes.

Moreover, if someone is unwilling to practice sexual self-discipline, think of other areas in one's life that might also be a struggle in self-control: emotions, food, language, exercise, entertainment. "We are what we repeatedly do. Excellence, then, is not an act but a habit."[12] Habits of self-control benefit a marriage, while a lack of self-control is selfish and damaging. Which marriage is more loving: a marriage where each partner serves himself or herself first and the spouse second, or a marriage where each spouse puts the other first? Sex is just one element of a loving marriage, and a couple's sexual relationship often reflects the relationship as a whole. Strive for a relationship that's sacrificial and self-giving. Give yourselves a wedding night to remember, not just another time of going to bed together.

---

11. *Catechism of the Catholic Church*, no. 1642.

12. Will Durant, *The Story of Philosophy: The Lives and Opinions of the World's Greatest Philosophers* (1926) (Simon & Schuster/Pocket Books, 1991), 98.

I'm not saying this to scare you into waiting for marriage. The title character of Edith Wharton's novel *Ethan Frome* cheats on his wife with her cousin, and he and the cousin both end up paralyzed in a sledding accident. Hello, scare tactic. (Edith Wharton: the *Mean Girls* Sex Ed teacher of 1911?) But chastity isn't about fear. Sometimes saving sex for marriage comes off as a series of "nos" that can lead you to live in constant fear of messing up. (I once saw an awkward skit where a husband and wife were supposed to give each other a brand new pair of shoes on their wedding night. But when they opened the boxes, the shoes were broken in and covered in dirt. You are *not* a dirty pair of shoes.) Chastity does you one better.

It's not saying "no" but saying "yes": "yes" to putting the one you love ahead of yourself, "yes" to love instead of lust (which is not the same as passion). Anyone can start doing that today, no matter where he or she has been. That's the beauty of chastity: you can always start over, virgin or not. It's not just about sex, so it doesn't end in marriage. Living a pure, chaste, authentic life has such power to heal and restore, and will spill over into every part of how honest and real you are in every interaction, how you see yourself and how you love your spouse. Sleeping together while you're still engaged "is not a matter of 'peeking under the wrapping paper.' It is a matter of completely missing the point of sex and marriage."[13]

Starting Over: God's Mercy Is So Much Bigger

No one is perfect at walking the walk—not your marriage prep instructors, not virgins, not mortifying sex-ed teachers. With all

---

13. Catholic Answers, "Cohabitation: Should We Live Together?" http:// www.chastity.com/article/cohabitation-should-we-live-together.

this talk of why chastity is so wonderfully worth it and why Church teaching is what it is, past wounds and regrets might be coming to the surface. Don't let them define you.

If you've made mistakes or have been hurt by sexual sins, know that it's never too late for you to embrace chastity and healing. Only God knows where you've been, and only he knows your heart. God's not angry with you. No. He wants so desperately for us, his children, to know his love and forgiveness.

God's not a God of grudges but of mercy. Compared to the ocean of God's mercy, our sin is barely a tiny drop. When we come back to him, he doesn't shake a finger at us; God rejoices and wants nothing more than to pour out his love. Don't let Satan rob you of the forgiveness that's rightfully yours for the asking. Stare down your fears and your past, and go to the Lord in Confession.

I know how intimidating it can be to confess, especially if it's been ages since you last knelt down in that box. But I also know firsthand the exhilarating sense of freedom that comes with the words, "may God give you pardon and peace, and I absolve you from your sins in the name of the Father, and of the Son, and of the Holy Spirit." Every single time, the peace that follows Confession is so much bigger than the embarrassment I felt going in.

Many times, guilt over past mistakes would make me feel restless and unsettled. I invite you to just rest: run to God's mercy, and forgive yourself, too. You'll fall again. Go to God again, every time, and know that rest. If you're asking why you have to tell your sins to a priest rather than just ask for forgiveness in your heart, know that in Reconciliation, the priest acts *in persona Christi*, literally in the person of Christ. Sacramentally, that means it's not your parish priest you're talking to in the confessional but Jesus himself. Nothing is more powerful. His forgiveness is real, and each time you're absolved from your sins, the path between your soul and God is perfectly clear. That pathway, free from sin, becomes an avenue for so many graces as you pursue chastity and a deeper love.

Sexual Healing

If you've suffered because of someone else's sexual sin, know foremost that in God's eyes you are perfect and whole. Healing from rape or sexual abuse of any kind is an immense process, one that's long and painful, yet it can be suffused with grace. (See Appendix C for resources.)

The Biggest Day of Your Life, Followed By the Biggest Night: Advice for First-Timers

It seems to me that among our generation, there's plenty of talk about sex in a general sense, both in the Church and in the culture, but not a lot of discussion about the nitty gritty of loving. Mostly due to grace, my husband and I were virgins at the altar, and though we weren't nervous, there are still a few things I wish someone had told me ahead of time. This is my very humble attempt to shed some light.

Pray. This might sound obvious, but bring your wedding night to prayer, especially if you're feeling shy or apprehensive. Ask the Lord to cast out your fear. Ask him to bring parts of your heart to light that might need healing or reorienting. It's different for everyone, but when I consider it, I attribute my sense of joyful anticipation and no fear at all to the theology of the body.

You did read that theology of the body section earlier in the chapter, right? To recap here, as well as offer a few new essentials, some of the late, great Pope's basic ideas are these: our sexuality is who we are and how we are created as men and women, and the fall caused the disordered view of sex that has brought some so much heartache. But, when we strive to love purely, holding nothing back and desiring nothing but to revere, not to use, the other person, we can get back a piece of the Garden as it was meant to be. No shame. Married love is only a tiny image of the awesome divine love of the Trinity. Amazing, isn't it? This only scratches the surface. I really have come to believe that viewing marriage and love through this lens has tremendous power to heal many wounds and to help one approach sex with joy and trembling, in the best sense.

But don't take yourselves too seriously. All the prayer and the theological ideas are great, but they don't have to be running through your head every second—it's your wedding night! While there's definitely the "head" aspect of sex that sees the bigger divine picture—that is certainly beautiful and worth contemplating—don't forget the "heart" aspect, too. A more earthly, sensory, and emotional experience is also going on. That's such a good thing!

God created sex, and if everything he created is inherently good, then of course sex is good. The body is good. Pleasure is good. Enjoy each other's beauty! God rejoices in a husband and wife delighting in one another, so don't put too much pressure on yourself to see your first night together as just singing choirs and flapping angel wings. Yes, a spiritual reality is taking place, but strive to be present in the earthly one, too.

Be patient with each other. Just like it takes time to build emotional, spiritual, and physical intimacy at the beginning of your relationship, it also takes time, we discovered, to adjust to sexual intimacy. That makes so much sense in hindsight. Magazines make it seem that if you're simply attracted to each other, then your sex life will instantly be blissfully complication-free. We found it so important, though, to talk honestly as we began to know each other in a new way. In my opinion, vulnerability and honest communication are what simplify things, and the natural attraction you already feel will follow. It's okay, and good, in fact, to talk about what feels good, what you like, what hurts or isn't comfortable, and even what turns you on (physically or otherwise). Honesty is sexy, right?

Try not to view sex in terms of rules. An engaged friend told me before her wedding that she felt strange going from being unmarried one day, when abstinence is a priority, to being married the next, when it's suddenly not. I understand the anxiety—it can seem like there's not much difference between unmarried and married than just some words and a big party. If you're feeling this way, I'd encourage you to contemplate the sacramentality of marriage. It literally transforms your relationship into a bond breakable only by death. Pray, also, to see sexuality as more than a set of rules. True, abstinence ends in marriage, but chastity doesn't. Chastity is all about ordering sexual desire properly so that you aren't enslaved to it. So it's natural that marriage brings a different approach to desire, but as long as purity and respect are present, sexual desire is nothing more or less than a new expression of the same love that's always been there.

Another word about rules. The Church requires that every marital embrace be both unitive and open to life (though not necessarily resulting in a new life each time). That said, it can feel tricky to navigate a new sense of freedom when it comes to married love and certain acts. There can be questions: "Is this okay?" "Is that?" and "Did we mess up?" While it's true every sexual act requires that the husband climax only during intercourse, you might be surprised to find there are few other directives about what's permissible. So long as both individuals feel that their dignity is being honored, and so long as the climax rule is upheld, very little is off limits. Be open to new things, talk about them, and pray together.

By the way, I highly recommend the book *Holy Sex* by Dr. Gregory Popcak, who discusses the nature of sex in a theological, but approachable voice, and includes extensive sections on the more technical, physical details of lovemaking in a reverent way.

And Not First-Timers

What if you're bringing something different to your marriage? If you've had sex before, or if you've been hurt in some way, know that there's nothing—*nothing*—that the Father's mercy and the graces of marriage can't ultimately heal. Even if you and your fiancé have already slept together, you can choose right now to save the next time you make love for your wedding night. It's a bold choice, one that takes guts, but the reward is worth the wait. One bride shares her experience:

> Eleven years ago, right up until the hotel door closed behind us on our wedding night, I would have laughed at the idea of being a born-again virgin. I would have said you either are or you aren't. Period. And yet, we made a decision. Although my husband and I had been sexually involved from early in our dating relationship, we spent almost our entire two-year engagement abstaining. I had been using the pill as contraception and became very worried that it would fail and I would get pregnant before our wedding, disappointing my parents beyond measure. So, for two years we abstained—well, we abstained from intercourse, but we were not chaste. Yet we felt the excitement of our wedding day—knowing we would finally be together again, the giggles of uncertainty as we left our friends and family to continue the party well into the night. We felt the joy of laughter as we removed over one hundred hairpins from my hair because I

couldn't lie down with them, and the joy of rediscovering one another. But this time it wasn't something we weren't supposed to be doing. It wasn't something "sinful" or "naughty" or "bad" or "dirty." It was exactly what we were supposed to be doing. It was beautiful and tears came as we lay together afterward, tears of joy, of love, of hope in the life that lay before us. And in those moments, I understood what being a born-again virgin was all about. As we got to know one another again in the coming months, we found things to be easier, less about pleasure and more about connecting than they had been prior to marriage.

If one or both of you has been with someone else, it will take an act of will and prayer to remove that person from your memory. Sexual intercourse, on many levels—spiritual, relational, emotional, biological—is meant to be with one person only, forever. It takes effort to break ties that are formed, ties that you have buried deep. Be patient and gentle with yourself and your fiancé.

Free, Faithful, Total, and Fruitful: How Contraception Limits Love

Born and raised Catholic, I learned somewhere along the way that the Church teaches contraceptives go against God's plan for marriage and the family. Until I started attending my church's youth group in high school, though, I thought contraception was one of those things that wasn't really taken seriously anymore.

I've discovered, as it turns out, that birth control (by which I mean all hormonal or barrier methods of contraception) is serious business. If love is meant to be free, faithful, total, and fruitful, it's meant to be given without reserve, to be promised and sealed in fidelity, to hold back nothing, and to invite a man and woman to become creators of new life. It all made a lot of sense, especially when I discovered the Catholic Church didn't insist that every sexual act produce a baby.

My understanding has since deepened beyond the sense of mere obedience that I understood as a high schooler. The more I learned, the more convinced I became that birth control is one of the greatest stumbling blocks in the way of romance, intimacy, and true freedom. I've become convinced that biologically, practically, logically, and even romantically speaking, keeping contraceptives out of your relationship can only foster deeper trust, honest communication, and authentic love. It's a love the human heart aches to be filled with.

I know I can't be the only one who's gotten on the kale, coconut oil, and organic cleaning-products train—magazines and the internet are practically rampant with the benefits of things like green juice, grass-fed everything, and alternative medicine. Yet with all the justified concerns we have about our well-being and environmental impact, so many of us seem to overlook a critical area of our lives: our reproductive health. Biologically, the birth control pill and other hormonal contraceptives work by releasing large amounts of synthetic hormones, estrogen and progestin, which suppress ovulation and mimic the hormonal symptoms of pregnancy. In other words, they fool a woman's body into a sort of state of constant pregnancy.

It's normal to take medicine when you have a headache. It's not normal when you don't. In the same way, the pill is marketed to "treat" a condition that doesn't exist: it's intended to actually prevent a healthy woman's body from functioning as it naturally does.

What's more, the information packet for the pill contains an extensive list of side effects directly related to taking it, ranging from weight gain, acne, migraines, and high blood pressure to heart attack and increased chances of breast and cervical cancer.

The pill often lowers a woman's sex drive, as well, which is ironic considering that sex is the reason for going on the pill in the first place. While packets are quick to point out that the pill is merely "associated with" higher instances of serious conditions, and that they are rare, I still personally don't find that the freedom to enjoy sex without pregnancy outweighs these risks.

I get so angry when I see how readily the pill is pushed on women, usually in the name of profit. Friends have told me that being on birth control is like feeling trapped in your own body, not feeling at all like yourself, and living in fear of what might happen to your complexion, weight, and future children if you ceased to take it. We deserve so much more. The health-related shortcomings of contraceptives speak for themselves, but the logical case against them is just as convincing.

Free, faithful, total, and fruitful. Even to someone who isn't religious, these four elements of love and sex are, at some point in a relationship, very desirable. Most would agree that the body speaks a language—it professes who we are and inspires complete self-gift—and that sex and love speak the same thing, whether it's intended or not. They say, "I want you, and all of you, forever." They're words we're all desperate to hear.

If one of these elements is missing, the body essentially speaks a lie. I want you, it says, but not all of you. It's a conditional promise. When the fruitful aspect of sex is artificially eliminated, fertility and its responsibilities are withheld and, along with them, a part of yourself.

Choosing to forego birth control in my marriage comes down to love. Cardinal Karol Wojtyla, the man who became Saint Pope John Paul II, wrote that the opposite of love is not hatred but using another person. Just a glance at the culture conveys that hookups, friends with benefits, and cohabitation have left so many of us broken. We're promised freedom but are left with deep wounds instead. No one's body or heart is meant to be used only for what it can offer sexually; it's meant for love that knows the entire person.

Each of us is so much more than just a body, but in our humanness this can be easy to forget. Even in a loving marriage, it's possible to desire one's spouse for self-gratifying purposes rather than from a desire to express love for the other. When birth control takes pregnancy off the table, I can only foresee a greater temptation to use one's spouse, even unintentionally, and to take sex for granted. Contraception could easily become a crutch to mask a lack of self-control. It's a daily battle to let love prevail over lust.

Every couple deserves the best possible chances of winning that battle.

Natural Family Planning

There's a better, more fulfilling way. During our engagement, Andrew and I signed up for Natural Family Planning (NFP) courses to prepare for a contraceptive-free marriage. NFP is a scientifically based, completely natural way of simply tracking, rather than altering, the existing conditions of a woman's body in order to determine periods of fertility and infertility throughout her cycle. A couple can use these observations to achieve or postpone pregnancy, abstaining if necessary for the week or so each month when the woman is most fertile. When used correctly, NFP is as effective at postponing pregnancy as the pill.[14]

---

14. See Frank-Herrmann, P., et al., "The Effectiveness of a Fertility Awareness Based Method to avoid pregnancy in relation to a couple's sexual behavior during the fertile time: a prospective longitudinal study," http://humrep.oxfordjournals. org/content/22/5/1310.long.

In our attempts to not take sex for granted, we've found NFP a powerful way to understand sex as good and beautiful without idolizing it. I'd be lying if I said it wasn't hard at first not to giggle when we learned that (prepare yourself) cervical mucus was one of the observable signs of fertility. We discovered that planning to use NFP in the abstract and actually sitting in a classroom learning it, trying to pretend a couple wasn't standing there talking about ovulation the way most people talk about the weather, are two completely different things. Remarkably, you get used to it.

It's actually something I'm thankful for. I'd venture that, between texting about my mucus while I'm at work, noting my fertility signs on a chart together each night, and constantly discerning a prudent time to grow our family, my husband and I have a more goofy, more intimate, and more joyful sex life than we ever could with birth control. The responsibility of planning our family doesn't just fall to me as I take a pill or replace a ring or a patch; it's shared by both of us. The self-control required to abstain during times of fertility sets us free to truly give ourselves to one another.

I know what you're thinking. What if your wedding night falls during a fertile time of your cycle and you've decided to postpone pregnancy? The thought that abstaining would be a total buzzkill is understandable, and is one that went through my head a few times as well. Speaking from experience, I can unreservedly say that not being able to have sex wasn't disappointing at all and didn't take one thing away from our wedding night. If you're anxious about the night not being special because you'll be abstaining, I'd encourage you not to view sex as a finish line. Strive, instead, to see every act of intimacy as something beautiful in and of itself, not just a step on the path to something else. Each one then becomes an act of love that isn't grasping for anything more beyond the present moment. After all, do you *want* your wedding night to be about just hustling to a finish line for your own enjoyment or about the electric joy to be found in each other along the way?

Intimacy isn't a right to be demanded. It's the fruit of loving, willful surrender. And sexual freedom doesn't mean a total lack of responsibility for each other. It means a willful choice to love in a pure, self-giving way.

If you are using contraception, I respectfully encourage you to stop using it. Take advantage of the NFP resources your diocese offers, or start with the resources in Appendix C. If you've been prescribed the pill as treatment for a medical condition, seek a second opinion from a naturopath or Catholic doctor.

I know that after years of magazine ads, doctor visits, and the culture presenting birth control as the only guarantee for preventing pregnancy, not using it feels so scary. NFP is a radical departure from our contraceptive culture. I can't say I know the ways of providence, but I can promise you choosing NFP will repay you in unimaginable ways. You'll experience incredible rewards in your health, your emotional well-being, your intimacy as a couple, and your entire marriage. That isn't because NFP solves every problem, but because when you live out your sexuality as God intends, you are that much more open to the grace he intends for every marriage, graces he wants to pour abundantly over your relationship.

The Problem with Porn

The human person is extraordinarily made, body and soul, and fulfills a specific purpose: to love and be loved. People are meant to be loved; things are meant to be used. Porn gets it backward. When people are used only for visual and sexual pleasure, they are literally dehumanized—the viewer no longer sees people as human but rather as sexual objects who exclusively exist to provide pleasure. The body is on display, yet the soul, the will, the intellect, and everything else that makes the person who he or she is, is obscured. Though porn obviously leaves nothing to the imagination, I'd argue that it actually doesn't even come close to revealing the fullness of the person.

Let me emphasize that porn isn't a problem because the body is a problem. Our bodies, made in God's image and likeness, are incredibly good, but sin twists what is good. Porn, then, takes the beauty and dignity of the body and exploits it.

The numbers of both men and women who habitually view pornographic material are large and continue to increase.[15] Studies and surveys suggest that viewing porn makes both men and women more likely to fear their partner will be unfaithful, to struggle with enjoying real sex, to be more critical of their partner's body, and to attribute divorce to a porn habit. Porn is so accessible and such a powerful temptation; I get how difficult it can be to resist. Practically speaking, there *are* ways to break the habit and to protect your relationship.

First, know that you can always wipe the slate clean with Confession. Sin thrives in darkness and the feeling that you're the only one struggling. The Father is merciful and never wants shame and isolation for us. He wants us to know his forgiveness and the freedom it brings. Go to him as often as you need to.

Second, make a plan to help you kick porn to the curb. Set up a filter on your computer, enlist the help of friends and perhaps a spiritual director to keep you accountable, and join a support

---

15. See "Internet Porn By the Numbers," http://internet-filter-review.topten reviews.com/internet-pornography-statistics.html.

group if you feel porn is an addiction you can't break. And lastly, consider your spouse-to-be the best, most worthy motivation for breaking the habit. Looking at porn essentially says you're okay with viewing the body of someone you're not married to for your sexual gratification. Putting on a wedding ring won't automatically change that outlook. It will take strength to reject temptation and build the virtue of purity.

Above all, as serious a matter as pornography is, be gentle with yourself. Habits aren't formed overnight, nor are they broken over-night. But with God's grace, it *is* possible. Bring your lust and temptation to the Cross and ask Jesus to crucify them, to slay them, and to strengthen you in love. Any habit is built on repeti-tion: each time you refuse porn, you become stronger.

Be Healed. Be Free. Live.

Sex and love ultimately profess the same thing: complete devotion, passionate self-gift, total freedom, an invitation to life, the promise of forever, and a taste of heaven. According to Venerable Fulton Sheen, "there is for the Christian no such thing in marriage as choosing between body and soul or sex and love. He must choose both together."[16] Married love is an education, twenty-four hours a day, in loving more like God loves. A sex life that truly is free, faithful, total, and fruitful allows a couple to glimpse his love. Don't close your bedroom door to God. Invite him in and be amazed at the immense joy it will bear in your marriage.

---

16. Sheen, *Three to Get Married,* 31.

Reflect on this chapter not just in your head but in your heart. Theological matters are important, but your relationship and the specific way you and your fiancé relate to each other are just as valuable. Be open and real about your concerns, your pasts, and your hopes for your sexual relationship. Sorting through past hurts is a delicate business, yet it's one that, when met with love, can bring about tremendous healing and intimacy.

A favorite image of mine comes from the end of the film *Slumdog Millionaire*, where the two main characters, soul mates who've been separated after years of searching for and suffering for each other, are finally reunited. The man presses his lips to a scar on the woman's cheek, the remains of a knife-wound she endured months earlier. That moment speaks such beauty to me. Kiss one another's wounds, be healed, and let your love bring forth life.

❖ *From the Groom* ❖

The Paradox of Commitment

I only seriously dated a few people before finding Stephanie. Even with my limited dating experience, it very quickly became apparent to me that I had an incredible desire to marry Stephanie. Earlier relationships often included inner conversations with myself amounting to "Yeah, I guess I could see myself marrying this girl," but with Steph, it was more like, "Holy smokes, I can't wait to marry this girl!"

Culturally, commitment isn't seen as comfort so much as confinement. But a virtuous commitment to a worthy person can, paradoxically, be one of the most freeing aspects of a relationship. Since Stephanie and I *chose* to join ourselves to each other, our commitment is an act of the will. There won't be any fears or worries about falling out of love because love is not just a feeling.

What makes commitment so paradoxical is that when you commit yourself to one person, when you make the choice to love that person without exception, when you say "no" to other sexual encounters (personal, pornographic, or otherwise), you are actually freeing yourself to love your spouse completely because you aren't chained to temptation and sin. I know my wife, and I love my wife, but I could always find ways to know or love her more. And through our committed love, I *want* to know and love her more because I know she is mine forever.

It's impossible to put into words the joy of knowing that every act of intimacy is a way of knowing my wife better. I'm free to fully love the person who fully loves me.

----- ❖ *For Conversation* ❖ -----

This chapter unpacks a lot: the Catholic understanding of sex and love, chastity, contraception, and Reconciliation, to name a few. Do any of these ideas challenge you? Talk about why, and in turn, I'd like to extend an invitation: if you remain unconvinced about any of these teachings, seek out a faithful friend and invite him or her to discuss them with you further.

Recall Saint Augustine's profession that "Our hearts are restless, O Lord, until they rest in thee." What aches have you felt in your heart? How have you experienced the restlessness he speaks of?

What, in your view, is the difference between abstinence and chastity? What does chastity look like before and after marriage?

Speaker Matthew Kelly says before you can give of yourself, you have to possess yourself—that is, a person can only love fully when he or she has developed self-control. Self-discipline might initially seem like a chain, but the reality couldn't be more different. Instead, when you have control over things like your emotions, sexuality, spending, and impulses, you become truly free: rather than being enslaved to your desires, you can discern which ones are good or harmful and can make a *choice* whether to act on them. Freedom is an essential part of love and self-gift.[17] How does chastity, which initially might seem like just a set of rules, actually open one to authentic freedom?

Married love is intended to be free, faithful, total, and fruitful. How does contraception inhibit these intentions for marriage, and how does rejecting contraception reflect these intentions?

What does Saint John Paul II mean when he says that "the problem with pornography isn't that it shows too much, but that it shows too little?"

Talking about sexuality, even in a reverent way, and discussing your future sex life can, well, light your fire, making chastity feel like a battlefield. Identify ways to openly, sensitively discuss your anticipations and anxieties in ways that don't cause temptation.

----

17. See Matthew Kelly, *The Seven Levels of Intimacy* (New York: Fireside, 2005), 62.

Chapter Eight
A Word from the Bridegroom

Note from Stephanie: You've been hearing stories and advice from my husband throughout this book. Here, in his own chapter, is an extended word from the man himself.

A Disagreeable Word

"REGISTERING." IT LOOKS like a pleasant enough word. It doesn't sound too bad either. It even ends on that rich-with-marriage-imagery syllable: "ring." In our experience, though, it sounded more like "bicker-ing."

Stephanie and I lived in different states during our engagement. We saw each other about one weekend a month, splitting the time between our families. I especially anticipated these times together. Because of the distance, we decided to attempt creating

141

and completing our wedding registry in one day. We were optimistic and determined. We were foolish.

We disagreed on a few "necessary" items. Stephanie didn't buy my argument that we should get the darkest shade of brown tablecloths because then we would only have to wash them every few months. I didn't buy her argument that we needed sixteen champagne flutes.

> *Andrew*: We haven't had champagne twice since we've met.
>
> *Steph*: We will when we are married!
>
> *Andrew*: Okay. Let's get two flutes?
>
> *Steph*: I suppose our grandkids will have to drink champagne from mugs on Christmas?
>
> (At the time of this conversation, we had zero kids, let alone grandkids.)
>
> *Andrew*: It's February. We have forty-five years and ten months before our grandkids are old enough to drink champagne with us on Christmas.
>
> *Steph*: I can't believe how coldhearted you are toward our grandkids.

Part of my frustration was that we were obligating our guests to buy things we didn't need just because it wasn't on our dime. It would have been nice to get those champagne flutes, but it would have been excessive. Your registry can be an exercise in self-control, an opportunity to discern what is a necessity and what is a frivolity. Doing so also honors your guests, treating them with respect for their budgets and not acting as if a wedding registry is an open checkbook.

But we weren't exactly being reflective at the time. Things escalated until we were disagreeing on *everything*. Forks without beaded handles? You must be out of your mind! A pricey kitchen mixer? It costs more than a laptop! By the time we left the store, our stomping did most of the talking.

Why Words Matter

Why embarrass ourselves with this story? I like to think it taught us something critical about communication. We had prided ourselves on our conversation skills. Since we were engaged long-distance, we spoke daily, often for a few hours at a time. Yet, when it came to disagreements, we were rookies. Here was an opportunity to discuss what was actually important to each of us.

It wasn't just that the tablecloth was darkly colored and therefore practical, but it was one of my favorite shades of brown; Stephanie called it ugly. It wasn't just that the mixer was useful; it was that, as Stephanie said later, its durability made it something sentimental we could pass on to our grandkids. Looking back, the grandkids-we-were-yet-to-have accidentally contributed to many of our disagreements.

The stereotype that women emote and men internalize can easily stifle an otherwise good opportunity for discussion. Of course, it's different for different couples. Some men really *do* struggle to put their feelings into words, and so do some women. Likewise, some men are much more comfortable expressing themselves, a trait commonly associated with women. But habits that mutually benefit a marriage, like communication or affection, shouldn't merely be relegated to one or the other gender.

Over dinner on the night of the registry battle, we slowly realized that even though we felt like we knew each other well, we still had many opportunities for misunderstanding. Without working to clarify things, we could have gone on much longer without speaking, fuming instead. That's not to say we've entirely overcome misunderstandings. It's just that we both consciously discuss times when we feel slighted or disrespected or hurt. It's not only foolish but presumptuous to assume that since I love Stephanie more than anyone, I suddenly understand her every thought and motivation. These conversations have steadily led toward a fuller understanding of my wife, a greater appreciation for who she is and how she loves. While I'll never claim to know her entirely, talking openly leads to both a deeper love and deeper knowledge of my wife.

Sometimes Not Communicating Is Communicating

I often come home from work so happy to be home, that where I hang my coat (*if* I hang my coat) is not at all important—that is, not important to *me.* Stephanie, happy to see me home, is also happy to see the coat hanging in the closet. She has told me this many times. Sometimes, while I am putting the coat away, she will again stress how important it is to hang up one's coat. And sometimes I respond sarcastically that that's a novel idea and I've never heard such insightful commentary on coat-hanging before.

Afterward, we're each embarrassed by our role in the argument (my snapping at Steph's repeated complaints, or vice versa on other days), and we either keep to ourselves, not acknowledging our pettiness, or we admit to our role in the unwarranted quarrel and apologize. On a good day, we'll choose the second action.

We have slowly learned that *not* voicing complaints, especially when those complaints are inconsequential in the long run, can be as beneficial (and honest) as saying them. Perhaps this is trite, but it's worth remembering, especially when it comes to bringing up critiques that don't contribute anything helpful or worthwhile. My wife is my best friend. Why would I want to spend some of our

time together fruitlessly criticizing her? How much more beneficial to spend that time enjoying her company and not nit-picking
all the things I think she does wrong.

This certainly gets dicier when one considers that "the sacrament of Marriage is the specific source and original means of
sanctification for Christian married couples and families."[1] This
means that, as Stephanie's husband, it's my responsibility to help
her get to heaven, and vice versa. Both of us have the responsibility
to do this for our children as well. This puts criticisms into a new
light. When she critiques my laziness in not putting my coat away,
is she actually trying to build the virtues necessary for me to get to
heaven? It's hard to say. But the very act of doing what my wife
wants—even if I do not give two hoots about putting my coat in
the closet—is the sort of virtuous self-denial, the ability to put my
wife's desires and needs above my own, that is critical to marriage.

Communication relies on honesty and on prudence, that virtue of good judgment by which one is thoughtful and careful. If it
bothers Stephanie to see a coat on the couch (or on the floor, or on
the table, or elsewhere), it's important for her to say so. But it also
takes prudence to sometimes *not* say so. Is it necessary that my wife
washes dishes in the exact same order I do? No. So I probably
shouldn't mention it to her. Obviously, the degree to which these
quirks bother someone will vary, but it's quite important to determine whether or not they are even worth discussing. The things
that aren't spoken can help your relationship just as much as the
things that are spoken.

---

1. John Paul II, *Familiaris Consortio*, no. 56 (Boston: Pauline Books & Media,
1981).

A Word on Love

The word *love* brings to mind many words, but I want to mention one specific definition of love, a definition I never heard until my twenties. It's a definition that entirely reshaped how I looked at marriage and sacrifice. Saint John Paul II said that to love is to will the good of another person. It's not just a religious idea. From Harry Potter to one of my favorite bands, The Strokes, our culture lauds sacrificial love, an act of self-denial done especially for the beloved because it is better for him or her. My constant priority should be what is best for Stephanie, even if it's not what's best or most convenient for me. Beautiful. But in practice, this is tough stuff.

First, my own desires sometimes get in the way. It's easy to explain away my lack of effort, to say, "I'll help her make dinner just as soon as I finish grading these last two papers," or "I'll take care of the baby this afternoon so she gets an afternoon off. But let me just finish my reading for class first." And those are my more noble excuses. Still, they're excuses, examples of conflicting desires that interrupt my responsibility to will the good of my wife.

At the same time, willing Stephanie's good can be a humbling experience for *her* as well. Not long after we got married, we were running late for Mass, and Stephanie was putting on makeup in the mirror, at home, at the time we should have already been at church. After applying one bad coat of mascara, then wiping it off, reapplying it, finding it unsatisfactory again, and beginning to *re*-reapply it, I tried to gently remind her that, in regard to what is ultimately best for her, being able to go to Mass (even while less-than-perfectly mascara-ed) was worth the short-lived embarrassment.[2]

---

2. I'm not saying it's unimportant to put effort into being presentable at Mass, but if it interferes with being fully and physically present, it's probably secondary to the Mass itself.

It's both hard to correct someone and hard to hear it, but as a husband, it's my responsibility to help my wife toward heaven, regardless of how difficult it is to do so. And it's her role to do the same for me. This sort of self-giving love is not for the faint of heart.

NFP and Other Sacrifices

It's impossible to talk about Natural Family Planning without talking about the sacrifice that comes with it. The most prominent example of this is physical intimacy, yet NFP isn't "all or nothing." There are still a number of ways to be intimate—loving acts that don't mimic sex or result in the husband's climax—even while abstaining.

The sacrifice required of each spouse is one of the most beautiful, and challenging, parts of NFP. It makes sacrifice such a natural part of marriage. Thankfully, the Church prepares us well for sacrifice: small acts of self-denial like fasting an hour before Mass, giving up certain desirable things in Lent, or sacrificing our time for prayer and works of charity.

In my own life, I notice a direct relationship between my ability to deny myself small things (like the last bite of cheesecake) to my ability to make larger sacrifices (like getting up to take care of the baby so Stephanie can sleep for a few hours). On the days when I continually indulge my appetites, I struggle to be as willing to sacrifice.

For me, my appetite for food is a strong indicator of my other appetites. When I lack self-control in the kitchen, I tend to lack it elsewhere. My go-to solution is to make small (*very* small) sacrifices with food: I'll prepare the food and then wait exactly ten minutes before eating it, I won't have sugar for the rest of the day, or I'll serve Stephanie the bigger, juicier burger without telling her. After doing this five or six times in a row, I've found it easier to deny myself in larger, more demanding tasks, both with food and otherwise.

Since NFP does call couples to discipline their sexual desires, it's helpful to be in the habit of readily sacrificing. Such an outlook can transform the weeks of abstaining from a chore to a joy. When we are postponing pregnancy, Stephanie and I certainly look forward to the days in her cycle when abstinence isn't necessary, but the rest of the month isn't spent in white-knuckled misery and sexual frustration. In fact, it's really shown us other, quieter ways of demonstrating love: cooking together, sneaking kisses (with both of us aware it isn't going to lead to sex), playing board games, going on walks, and generally loving with our words and actions, not just our bodies.

Sometimes we'll welcome romance with a fancy dinner and an at-home date. When we have champagne these days, we drink it out of normal wine glasses. We only have four of them. Our grandkids haven't complained about it yet.

❖ *For Conversation* ❖

What, do you think, is the root of the expectation that women emote and men internalize? Identify ways to push beyond these stereotypes and communicate your feelings.

Wedding preparation can unintentionally foster new forms of disagreement in your relationship. Talk about constructive ways to work through differences of opinion when it comes to planning your life together.

Why is it just as important to consider what's *not* said as carefully as it is to consider what *is* said? How can you cultivate mindfulness in the ways you speak to each other?

What's the difference between nitpicking and loving correction? Discuss ways to distinguish between the two and help lead each other to virtue in a way that's encouraging, not nagging.

Why do small sacrifices pave the way for larger ones? List several small daily sacrifices each of you can make for the sake of the other and for your relationship.

Chapter Nine
Starting Your Life Together

In INFINITE WAYS, life after the wedding is pure bliss: saying good night instead of goodbye before bed; knowing your dishes and towels and even your toilet paper belong not just to you but to both of you; new things to laugh about as a result of more time spent together. I don't mean to sound like a wet blanket, but realistically speaking, married life calls for countless practical adjustments besides the fun, sexy ones. It's normal to struggle with some of these adjustments. Happily, though, you have a lifetime to work through them. Read on for how to deal with some common surprises and trials of newlywed life.

Your Honeymoon: And Facebook Makes Three?

I fully admit to the need to take excessive photos on my honeymoon so as to give people the impression that we didn't just spend the whole time in bed. And yet, I suspect that's not the overwhelming reason behind the times I see people's honeymoon pictures popping up every ten minutes on my screen.

The main point of your honeymoon is to immerse yourself in the presence of your new husband or wife. Social media-fying it to death is like immersing yourself in the presence of your new spouse *and* your 200 followers. A lot can be said, in my opinion, about veiling those first days of your marriage in a little mystery, and about the peace that comes from not hearing dozens of notifications pop up on your phone all day.

No matter where you've been and what you're bringing to your marriage, your honeymoon brings something newly intimate. The two of you are the only people in the world who will experience it in its fullness, and the depth of that fullness you share takes on a sacredness. It's like the best kind of secret.

So by all means, take photos of your cocktails and your rings and your toes in the sand, but before immediately sharing photos, ask yourself: (a) what is your underlying reason for taking the photo in the first place (is it purely to express your joy or to see how many Likes it will get?), and (b) will sharing it help you relax and be present to your spouse? Make your honeymoon a getaway in the true sense of the word: seriously consider a media-free trip, or at least a minimal-media one, by putting down your phone—I doubt you'll miss it—and being possessive of the time you have with just each other.

Getting Over Yourself: Modeling Your Marriage on Franciscan Values

Christ sanctified his bride, the Church, and opened up heaven so we could have eternal life. He did it at no small cost: by hanging on a cross. Even in moments of deepest despair, crying out, "My God, my God, why have you forsaken me?" (Mt 27:46), Jesus gives of himself completely, suffering purely out of love for us. His crucifixion and death are anything but self-serving. They're completely self-giving.

That gift of self is on tap for us, too, through grace. Saint Francis of Assisi said, "Above all the grace and the gifts that Christ gives to his beloved is that of overcoming self." Francis' spirituality was rooted in three promises: poverty, chastity, and obedience. Franciscan religious orders still take these vows today, but you don't have to run off to a monastery to implement these promises into your life. In fact, they provide a phenomenal foundation for the vocation of marriage, as well.

Poverty: At Least There's No Salad on the Walls

I spent a good chunk of my teenage years watching reruns of the sitcom *Boy Meets World*. In one of my favorite episodes, Cory and Topanga, childhood sweethearts who are finally married, move into their first apartment. Mud comes out of the faucet, everyone tells them they're on their own, and both the dried remains of a salad and a bullet hole are found on the wall. After a few weeks of arguments, bad hygiene, and bouts of envy at their friends' cushy living situations, the newlyweds ultimately determine they need to make their own happiness, rather than measuring their satisfaction in apartments and income. They even figure out how to fix the faucet. Cory's mom is proud of him. She recalls the start of her own marriage, being young and poor, calling it the hardest but sweetest time of their lives.

Life, of course, doesn't come with neatly scripted endings. We got married the summer after Andrew's first year of grad school. I'd just completed a year of service, with no future job prospects yet, and moved to the college town four hours from home where he was studying. During the eight months of unemployment that followed, I occasionally recalled that episode and cursed its triteness. Being poor and on our own did *not* feel warm, fuzzy, and romantic most of the time. We'd just received pristine white bath towels and a food processor with four different chopping attachments but would split meals when our friends invited us out to dinner. Andrew found us a great apartment, but we didn't turn the heat on until November because we wanted to keep our bills down.

And yet, a few years later, looking from the other side of those early days, I treasure that time of transition. My husband and I had the privilege of plenty of time together, the thrill of discovering our adopted town, and the test of virtue that came with trusting in God's faithfulness. I know that's always the sort of thing people say, and I am quite aware that we were spoiled in our situation, compared to some others. I honestly can say, though, I'm not disappointed that things weren't easy to come by at first. I feel like it's made our marriage a truly shared life, since we've gotten on our adult feet together, rather than having done that separately. Everyone's story is different, but in our case of marrying young while still in school, there are no regrets.

This doesn't mean your marriage is less noble if you have two incomes and maybe even a house from the get-go. Nor do I think you're guaranteed to struggle more if you are starting out with a tougher financial situation. It's not a competition. Regardless of how much you have in the bank, I encourage you to live your marriage with a spirit of poverty.

It's about so much more than money. Poverty of spirit is emptying yourself, not for the sake of emptiness alone, but to make some room for the Lord. When we come to him as beggars, depending entirely on his grace and love, God fills our longing hearts. Love for us is his joy: "For you know the generous act of our Lord Jesus Christ, that though he was rich, yet for your sakes he became poor, so that by his poverty you might become rich" (2 Cor 8:9).

What does poverty look like in daily married life? Apologizing quickly instead of holding grudges, admitting when you've messed up, developing a shared prayer life, reminding one another to trust in God when the going gets rough, and being content with what you have are ways to develop a heart of poverty.

Chastity: Control of the Self for Love of the Other

Abstinence ends in marriage, but chastity doesn't. It encompasses so much more than the sex you're having or not having. Chastity does, however, involve sexual self-control and an abiding regard for your spouse as a man or woman created in God's image. That means seeing him or her as some*one* to be loved and not some*thing* to be lusted after. Practically speaking, it means doing thoughtful and special things for your spouse outside the bedroom, rejecting porn and degrading jokes, and being understanding when your husband or wife isn't in the mood, remembering that "if we respect desire within love, we will not violate love."[1]

If you're reading this book cover to cover, you just read a few thousand words about chastity in regard to sexuality, so I won't repeat them here. Keep in mind, though, that chastity's underlying

---

1. From a letter by Karol Wojtyla, as excerpted in George Weigel, *Witness to Hope* (New York: Harper Collins, 1999), 98.

principles, self-control and mutual respect, are also integral to a relationship in other ways. Maintaining control and practicing moderation in any one area of your life, whether it's your emotions, language, eating and drinking, spending, or sexuality, amplifies your ability to apply the same virtues to other areas. Chastity just keeps on giving, quite literally: the more possession you have over yourself and your desires, the freer and abler you are to give of yourself in love.

Obedience: Love Like the Cross

One of the more controversial Scripture passages is from Saint Paul's Letter to the Ephesians: "Wives, be subject to your husbands as you are to the Lord. For the husband is the head of the wife just as Christ is the head of the church, the body of which he is the Savior. Just as the church is subject to Christ, so also wives ought to be, in everything, to their husbands" (5:22–24). Before you write off Saint Paul, hear me out and have a look at what comes before this passage and what follows it. Consider, for a moment, what Paul is really saying.

The verse immediately preceding Paul's instruction to wives states, "Be subject to one another out of reverence for Christ" (Eph 5:21). To *one another*. This verse, to me, makes it clear that a husband's and wife's relationship isn't about one spouse dominating every decision while the other spinelessly nods along. Both spouses humble themselves and seek to obey and respect each other.

What's more, they're not doing it only for each other or because they're supposed to, but "out of reverence for Christ." It's realizing your own ways aren't necessarily the best or most important ones. Dying to yourself, sacrificing your own will even when it's hard or when you don't want to—in matters as simple as where to go out for dinner or as major as whether to change careers—is a daily measure of obedient love.

The verse that follows sometimes gets forgotten because people tend to become so contentious as soon as Paul tells the wives what to do. Incidentally, it's the husbands' turn next. "Husbands, love your wives, just as Christ loved the church and gave himself up for her, in order to make her holy by cleansing her with the washing of water by the word, so as to present the church to himself in splendor, without spot or wrinkle or anything of the kind—yes, so that she may be holy and without blemish" (Eph 5:25–27).

It sounds great, Christ giving himself up for the Church, cleansing and purifying his bride, and it really is. It's also exhausting, bloody, and excruciating; the fruit of a relentless, heroic love. The Church is "subject to Christ" in the sense that she willingly receives all of the love Jesus freely gives on the cross. The bride's very act of receiving is an act of love.

So how to give love, receive love, and obey? Let your spouse pick the movie tonight. Give him or her the biggest piece and the last bite of dessert. Let her make her case first next time you disagree about something, and really listen instead of just mentally practicing for when it's your turn to talk. Do the things he asks you to do (get him a glass of water, pick up eggs on the way home, dig tomorrow's khakis out of the dryer) quickly and well. Obedience isn't sexist, it isn't old-fashioned, and it isn't weak. It's radical, sacrificial love.

Moving in Together, or How I Found Out There Is Such a Thing as Bachelorette Towels

Living out your wedding vows through poverty, chastity, and obedience is not for the wimpy. After our wedding, I quickly found out marriage is a daily training ground in love, which is a good thing even when it's painful. Like the time I realized living for another person, and not just myself, isn't always in the big picture but in the details.

By nature, wedding gifts are, of course, gifts, and they deserve to be appreciated as such, since no one's *required* to give you anything. I suppose, though, it's not uncommon for newlyweds to need to return a few items here and there, or to fill in the gaps of their new nest with additional purchases.

I'd venture that it *is* uncommon for newlyweds to frequently return items they themselves have bought. Yet there I found myself, flamingo-pink towels in hand, at a return counter, and not for the first time. I liked not having a job lined up when we first got married. It gave me plenty of time to adjust to a new area, relax after the chaos of our wedding, and to engage in my new favorite pastime—organizing and decorating our new apartment.

Our new apartment. While Andrew was off reading literary theory and instructing America's young minds in the ways of the independent clause, I craved a sense of purpose amid seemingly endless job applications and half-finished books and craft projects. Consequently, I found myself enjoying errands to an unusual degree, and even inventing reasons to go out to do them. My wandering habits resulted in more than a few impulse buys in the interest of furbishing; buys I genuinely liked, but impulses all the same. Are you noticing, by the way, how many times I'm using "I" and "my?"

I bought some frames for wedding photos and a little sponge holder on suction cups to keep in the kitchen sink. "Oh, good idea," said Andrew. I found an organic all-purpose cleaning solution that smelled deliciously of real lavender and could be diluted into what equaled dozens of uses. "Did you have to get the expensive one?" he asked. I brought home a large coral sculpture and proceeded to artfully arrange it with books and candles on our coffee table. "I don't think we really needed a giant piece of sea life," he said (I was unemployed, remember, and he was making a shoestring graduate salary).

We hit the breaking point with the pink towels. As I waved them excitedly, my husband said, "Those look like they belong in a trendy bachelorette apartment." I teared up, then huffed away (Present Stephanie to Past Stephanie: you were ridiculous). Didn't he *want* a trendy apartment? Didn't we need a little color in the bathroom? They had a clover print!

I cringe. After a fair amount of resistance to my heart being stretched, I realized something important. As happy as I was to finally be married, I was still living like a single lady. I had been spending my time how I liked, buying what I liked, and generally not consulting my husband on decisions that would affect both of us. I was quickly discovering that combining your lives and your entire selves in marriage also entails combining everything you own.

Marriage can easily be two people just doing their own thing in each others' orbits, side by side. Or it can be life lived face to face, in constant pursuit of the other's joy and holiness. I wanted that: a shared, united life where "our own thing" meant the both of us together, not each of us separately, towels and all.

A few years into marriage, I'm still learning, and sometimes fighting, what it really means to belong to another person and to live face to face. You don't reach a point where each person feels like they've loved enough, given enough, sacrificed enough, and can just coast for the rest of his or her days. You keep choosing to love, and in doing so your love is amplified. Sharing unselfishly, giving yourself fully, disagreeing and, just maybe, returning the things your husband doesn't like, with love? Those are the real wedding gifts.

If You're Relocating for Love

The thing I discovered about following my new husband to his grad school town is that there were only so many times I could arrange our books by color and wipe down the countertops. I felt guilty: here I was, so happy to be married. But the adjustment of going somewhere completely new with barely any connections or work prospects, and many days spent alone, very often felt burdensome. I didn't want Andrew to feel bad that I'd come with him to a place where I felt alienated.

Thankfully, we eventually made true friendships there, and after a few false starts on the job front, I was blessed with a position I enjoyed. But I remember so clearly the anxiety and restlessness I felt in the beginning. So, I respectfully offer you my advice on relocating after marriage, and believe me, it's advice gained much more in hindsight than during the experience. I wish I could have given these words of wisdom to myself!

Set a routine for yourself. I liked sleeping until 10:00 AM, but only for about three weeks. Then I felt frustrated by mindlessly whiling away my days. It took a good amount of willpower (and failed attempts), but I tried hard to wake up relatively early to my alarm and to treat exercise, job applications, reading, meal planning, and prayer as a schedule not as options. I asked Andrew to keep me accountable, and I also set a limit for myself on Internet time. Be gentle with yourself when you fall short.

Prioritize your spiritual life. Getting myself to the chapel for daily Mass ensured that I at least changed out of my pajamas most days. Mass was at the end of Andrew's workday, and I started looking forward to meeting him on campus and then our walking home together. What's more, idle time can be vulnerable time when it comes to spiritual warfare. I quickly noticed that when I neglected my prayer life, skipped out on the sacraments, or wasted my time, I found it much harder to trust in God, sense my worth, and sustain hope about our financial situation.

Go out. Seriously. We were trying to save money, and I have some introvert tendencies, so at first it was a little too easy for me to spend a lot of time on my own. Sometimes I didn't mind, but other times I wanted to pull my hair out. Luckily, as the months went by and we made friends at church and in my husband's program, socializing became easier. I discovered it was just a matter of actually hanging out with people even when I mistakenly thought they were all busier than me. On another level, physically going out the door most days helped my sanity in so many ways.

If you're the spouse who isn't relocating, but already lives in your future home: Get to know your town better in the months leading up to your wedding! Consider this time an excuse to sample a few new restaurants and sights in the name of research for future date nights. Get your friends excited to meet your fiancé when he or she joins you there. If you haven't found out for yourself yet, ask around to find the best places for an oil change, a haircut, a bike ride. Discovering places and people that you and your spouse will soon be experiencing together is a caring way to aid in the transition ahead.

A Universal Call to Holiness

Getting married Catholic inherently means signing up to bear God's love to the world. Marriage and the family are "willed by God in the very act of creation"[2] and "the sacrament gives [spouses]

---

2. *Familiaris Consortio,* 3.

the grace and duty of commemorating the great works of God and of bearing witness to them before their children."[3] Every vocation calls the faithful to holiness. Priests and sisters bear witness to the Gospel in a fairly public way, through their dress and their ministry, but they aren't the only ones called to become saints. Married couples also can, and should, witness to God's loving nature through the purifying, sanctifying love that flows from their gift of self and through raising their children in the Church.

So, how to create a home and a life together that rejoices in and reflects the Catholic faith? In a gift shop in Albuquerque, New Mexico, I saw a jewelry box bearing the Divine Mercy image of Jesus surrounded by mirrors and glittery butterflies. The red and white rays radiating from his hands were made of light-up fiber optics. Sometimes ridiculous stuff like that box, that Andrew and I named "Fabulous Jesus," comes to mind when one pictures living it up Catholic. But in fact, you can cultivate the love of Christ in your marriage, both at home and in the world, without a single butterfly in sight. Here are a few ways to do it:

- Go to Mass together as often as you can. When you have different work schedules and, eventually, kids, it can be tempting to go to Sunday Mass individually, at whatever times are convenient. But worshipping and receiving Jesus' Body and Blood together as a family is a profound experience. Even if it takes extra effort to go to the same Mass, it's worth the shared time spent together in prayer.

- Fast like a saint. Deny or challenge yourself daily for the good of your relationship, and offer your sacrifice for your

---

3. Ibid., 13.

spouse's holiness. Maybe wait until midmorning for your first cup of coffee, set a time limit on social media, leave the radio off when you're in the car, or offer every rep of your workout for a specific prayer intention. During Lent, keep each other accountable for your promises and pray together the Stations of the Cross.

❖ And feast like a saint. Live liturgically by celebrating holy days and different seasons of the Church calendar accordingly. Make a wreath and calendar for Advent, pray a novena (a prayer said over nine days) before a favorite saint's feast day, and invite friends over for a special meal on Marian feasts like the Immaculate Conception (December 8) or the Annunciation (March 25). With time, you'll build up plenty of traditions to share with your children and friends.

❖ Take it to the sin bin. Go to Confession together regularly. Keeping a clear relationship with the Lord encourages a clear relationship with each other.

❖ Designate an area of your home for shared prayer and contemplation. Nothing fancy: rosaries, a journal, Bible or other books for spiritual reading, and a religious image or sculpture are all you need. Using the space specifically for prayer helps remove you from your life's other distractions and encourages the habit of prayer. Pray together each day, even if it's just for a few minutes. Speaking of which . . .

Four Hands, One Heart: Praying Together

I didn't have much of anything resembling a prayer life until college. Even once I did, it took a long time to feel like prayer could be more like a casual conversation than a formal script. I knew the Lord loved me beyond all telling, yet, although I could say anything I wanted, I still felt self-conscious.

So I don't know why I was surprised when, if I felt shy around God, I also felt shy praying in front of Andrew when we first started dating. In the beginning, we took Rosary walks around our campus, hands in each other's coat pockets. I treasure that newness under the stars. Everything felt so right and so free. Nothing was weird about praying the Rosary together because all the words were predetermined.

It took ages though, until well after we were engaged, to feel the same level of comfort with more spontaneous prayer. When things get quiet or awkward, it's so easy to just say a Hail Mary rather than bare your soul. Prayer is an intimate, vulnerable way of communicating, maybe because you aren't communicating only with each other. Just like your emotional and physical intimacy develop gradually, however, spiritual intimacy also develops in a way that lets the Lord take his time.

There's no timetable and no single solution, so don't feel anxious about speaking or acting in a certain way if you've never prayed together before. More structured prayer is no less wonderful a way to bring Christ into your marriage. As you get used to it, you might find it gets easier to pray what's in your heart, out loud. With time, the prayer I shared with Andrew grew more conversational and personal, changing naturally as we fell more in love. Spending even a few minutes together in prayer each day seems to ground our relationship, help us deal with stress, and make forgiveness easier. Adding our intentions to each decade when we pray the Rosary; sharing our insights from Mass, adoration, and spiritual reading; and hearing Andrew's voice next to my ear as we pray before bed have become some of my most cherished rituals. It's romantic, too, to know your spouse in the way he or she talks to God—really! One prayer to the Holy Spirit asks the Lord to "enkindle in them the fire of thy divine love." Amen to that.

All the Joy and Sweetness Possible

In place of a guest book, we provided our wedding guests with blank note cards, asking them to write something special for us. We set out cards and pens with a list of questions for our family and friends, including, "What's the secret to an extraordinary marriage?" "What's the best and worst advice newlyweds receive?" and "What's your favorite dinner for two?" Some responses were too valuable not to share:

- "*Ad Jesu per Mariam*" (to Jesus, through Mary).
- "Don't expect a perfect honeymoon. Living together and seeing each other 24/7 takes some adjusting."
- "Take time to date your spouse."
- "Love means . . . honesty. The strength to endure it and the wisdom to appreciate it."
- "May the good Lord shine a light on you, make every song you sing your favorite tune. May the good Lord shine a light on you, warm like the evening sun."
- "Brush your teeth."
- "Laugh. Be honest. Be kind. Make time for each other and yourself. If anything creates a space or wall between you, reject it. Know that God is good. God loves you. God wants to give you all the joy and sweetness possible."

"All the joy and sweetness possible." That is my prayer for you. May you have peace in your heart as you prepare to walk up the aisle, and a long, fulfilling life, filled with abundant grace, as you walk out the doors of that church and start your life together. Don't worry, and if you do, look to Saint Maximilian Kolbe's complete reliance on Our Lady: "As for the future, I place all my trust in her."

--------- ❖ *From the Groom* ❖ ---------

Change Happens, and It's Good

Maybe I missed something obvious, but life after marriage was incredibly different than life before it. This changed even more dramatically after having a baby. My life went from a self-centric life, that isn't necessarily a bad thing for a bachelor—to an attempted—and often failed—wife-centric life, and now it's baby-and-family-centric.

While I absolutely love my married and family life, truth be told, I sometimes wonder what I would be up to if I weren't married, or what Stephanie and I would be doing with our evenings if they weren't spent trying to convince a baby that he shouldn't be eating his baby wipes and should instead go to sleep like a responsible infant. Without a doubt, it's a serious adjustment. Before, our relationship was concerned mainly with each other, but then our concerns for each other were placed in the context of parenthood. Our son is a part of our lives, a part of us, and a part of our relationship, just as Stephanie became a part of me in marriage and I a part of her.

Who we are now isn't who we were when we met, or even who we were when we married. This is true financially, locationally, physically, emotionally, spiritually, and just about every other way. Rather than dwell in the past, we try to see challenges as ways to help our relationship develop. We grow together, as a unified family. And we see our love growing along with us.

◈ For Conversation ◈

Drinks with umbrellas aside, what do you envision for your honeymoon and how you'll spend your time? Discuss the role social media plays in your relationship and how you'd like to utilize it, or not utilize it, on your first married trip together.

What images come to mind when you hear the words "poverty," "chastity," and "obedience"? How does love transform these seemingly austere, obligatory qualities into positive virtues that are freely chosen?

Compare a "side-by-side" relationship with a "face-to-face" one. What do their differences look like day to day?

Will your location or work situation change for either of you after you're married? Talk about any anxieties you might be experiencing and pinpoint practical ways to deal with them.

Identify ways to center your marriage on Christ and the Church. What religious traditions would you like to introduce in your married life?

What's your spiritual relationship like? Try praying together for five minutes every day for a week, any way you like, and spend some time sharing your feelings about shared prayer.

Acknowledgments

By the time I held my son, Aaron, for the first time, I'd spent twelve hours in labor and three and a half pushing. Writing a book, I found out, is not unlike labor: both are filled with false starts, disbelief in ever reaching the finish line, and frequent temptations to just curl up in a ball and cry. Yet at the end, in both cases, I've been amazed by God's generosity and abundant grace, full to overflowing with thanks. With love and deep gratitude, I thank:

- Captive the Heart readers for turning a humble, unknown piece of the internet into a slightly more known, hopefully still humble community. Thank you for your friendship, your honest hearts, and for sticking with a blogger who took an eleven-month maternity leave. Truly, you are a gift to me.

- The sisters and staff at Pauline Books & Media. I hope the words on these pages honor and reflect the hope you had for them. Sr. Christina Wegendt, I'm unimaginably grateful to you for approaching me with your idea for this book. For a girl who daydreamed in fourth grade of writing children's books, then let the idea drift off at some point, becoming a published author is a dream fulfilled. And thank you for making me aware of Track Changes. Sr. Marianne Lorraine, your wisdom and gentle persistence as an editor have humbled me, in the best way. Thank you so much for pushing back, with great charity, against my times of hardheadedness and helping clarify my writing into its most sincere, truthful, grammatically correct form. Vanessa Reese, securing permissions for the quotes used in this book was a project unto itself that gave me a taste of the work you do each day. Without a doubt, your expertise and hard work in the permissions corner of the publishing world far outweigh mine, so for that, and for answering my many, many questions, I'm thankful.

❖ My friends who never tire of answering and debating my theological questions. Jacob and Ashley King, I'm positive that some fruits of our three-hour dinner conversations have found their way into this book. We are forever thankful that you lassoed us into ministry with you, for all of those dinners, your example, your truest friendship, and for keeping Andrew's and my embarrassing stories mostly to yourselves. Jonathan and Siobhan Benitez, I'm fascinated, every time, by the energy and seriousness with which you entertain my inquiries about Scripture, Church history, metaphysics, the sacraments, and everything else related to them. In fact, I sometimes think you forget I'm watching and absorbing, and I get the pleasure of just watching two amazing minds work out an idea. Thank you for sharing your knowledge and for nearly a decade of friendship; I couldn't be happier that we are bound together, siblings in the Immaculata, for eternity. Thank you, also, for anything you have ever baked for me.

❖ Arleen Spenceley, I look up to your boldness, your way with words, and your rock-solid faith. I praise God for the timing of us both navigating this road to publishing together, and praise God for you being first so I could look to your example and not have to figure things out entirely on my own. Thank you for praying for me, asking me to pray for you, inviting me to write for your blog, answering my panicked e-mails and texts, and for those months I was writing my proposal when we spent most of our workdays chatting online.

❖ The precious family I gained from my year on mission, as you fully embrace your vocations and restore hope to the broken—that is, everyone—through Generation Life and The Culture Project. Your prayers, love, and tremendous virtue purify me and call me on to this day. True to our typical plundering of each others' stories, jokes, and examples, I know I've done so in these pages and am so inspired by and appreciative of your witnesses. Words fail me in the way I wish I could thank you. Long live nuptial union.

❖ The Augustine Institute, Theology of the Body Institute, and the man at the core of them both, Pope Saint John Paul II. Retreat highs fade, but if I've learned anything from the understanding of love I took home from my time in Allenspark and Quarryville, it's that love is so much more than an emotional high. I am radically, forever changed by the education I received in *Love and Responsibility* and the theology of the body. JPII, I know so clearly how much you have prayed with me and for me. Your teachings have been medicine for my soul and insistence to become passionately alive. Thank you, and one day I fully plan to run into your arms with my resurrected body.

❖ Andrew, never have I met a man so loving, so creative, so tender, and so sacrificial. And rarely have I seen your spirit of sacrifice so evident as when my writing deadlines were approaching and you took care of our family and our apartment in ways I couldn't. I'm in a constant state of wonder at how faithful God is and how richly God has blessed me with you for my husband. Until I wrote this book, I had no idea so many ways your rightness for me existed, not least of which include your willingness to sit and chat instead of doing the dishes on busy nights and to let me talk you into getting takeout when I had to keep working on everything. I am so undeserving of your love and service and plan to spend all the rest of my days loving you back in the way you are worthy of. Thank you, thank you, thank you.

❖ My babies. Aaron, you are so considerate for learning how to sleep through the night, finally, after thirteen months, in time for me to turn in my manuscript. I pray you grow into a man of virtue and strength (which, God willing, won't be so impossible with your dad as your model), a man who loves fully and fulfills his vocation in complete self-gift. And to your sister whom I haven't met yet, morning sickness couldn't stop your mama from editing her final draft. My hope for you, too, is virtue, deep faith, and that you see, every day, what an honest, loving marriage looks like. I love you both entirely.

Appendix A
The Catholic Rite of Marriage

It's pretty easy to find the Rite of Marriage online,[1] but I'm including it here because I refer to it so often in this book. Revisit this section often, meditate on the love and fidelity the two of you will promise to each other, and let the words sink in deep.

Address and Statement of Intentions

The priest addresses the couple before the congregation:

In the presence of the Church, I ask you to state your intentions.

(*Name*) and (*Name*), have you come here freely and without reservation to give yourselves to each other in marriage?

---

1. See Planning a Catholic Wedding—Rite of Marriage, copyright © United States Confraternity of Catholic Bishops, http://www.foryourmarriage.org/catholic-marriage/planning-a-catholic-wedding/rite-of-marriage/.

Each responds:
I have.

Priest:
Will you love and honor each other as man and wife for the rest of your lives?

Each responds:
I will.

Priest:
Will you accept children lovingly from God and bring them up according to the law of Christ and his Church?

Each responds:
I will.

Consent and Exchange of Vows

The priest invites the couple to declare their consent through their wedding vows:
Since it is your intention to enter into marriage, join your right hands, and declare your consent before God and his Church.

The bride and bridegroom join hands, and each says:
I, (*Name*), take you, (*Name*), to be my (*wife/husband*). I promise to be true to you in good times and in bad, in sickness and in health. I will love you and honor you all the days of my life.

Or

I, (*Name*), take you, (*Name*), for my lawful (*wife/husband*), to have and to hold, from this day forward, for better, for worse,

for richer, for poorer, in sickness and in health, until death do
us part.

*Note: You may choose which of these two forms of your vows to use. There are
also the options of having the celebrant guide you through your vows, repeat-
ing after him line by line, or of memorizing the words and speaking them in
their entirety, directly to one another.*

The priest says:

You have declared your consent before the Church. May the
Lord in his goodness strengthen your consent and fill you both
with his blessings.

What God has joined, men must not divide.

Response:

Amen.

Blessing and Exchange of Rings

The priest blesses the couple's rings, using one of these forms:

May the Lord bless these rings which you give to each other as
the sign of your love and fidelity.

Response:

Amen.

Or

Priest:

Lord, bless these rings which we bless in your name.

Grant that those who wear them may always have a deep faith
in each other.

May they do your will and always live together in peace, good will, and love.

We ask this through Christ our Lord.

Response:

Amen.

Or

Priest:

Lord, bless and consecrate (*Name*) and (*Name*) in their love for each other.

May these rings be a symbol of true faith in each other, and always remind them of their love. Through Christ our Lord.

Response:

Amen.

The bride and groom place the rings on one another's fingers, each saying:

(*Name*), take this ring as a sign of my love and fidelity. In the name of the Father, and of the Son, and of the Holy Spirit.

The Mass proceeds from here, beginning with the Creed. The sacrament is ratified through the Rite of Marriage and the Nuptial Blessing that concludes the Mass, and later on, the sacrament is sealed when the bride and groom consummate their marriage. Consummation renders their union indissoluble: literally, unable to be broken.

Appendix B
Special Circumstances

Each of the situations that follow are, ultimately, matters of pastoral guidance that should be given particular attention during your marriage prep and treated with love and sensitivity before and after marriage. Use this Appendix as an overview of the Church's position on several unique marital circumstances and an introduction to what to expect.

When One of You Is Catholic and the Other Is Not

If you and your fiancé are both Christians but not both Catholic, Church approval must be obtained for the wedding.[1]

---

1. See *Catechism of the Catholic Church*, nos. 1633–1637.

Your celebrant can tell you how to obtain the required approval from your diocese. This is called "permission to enter into a mixed marriage." "Mixed" here refers to the difference in religious faith. Bear in mind that, given the sacredness and permanence of marriage in the eyes of the Church, the spouse who is Catholic is making a promise, in his or her vows, to be responsible for raising children in the Catholic faith. He or she promises to sincerely commit to the Catholic faith through things like going to Sunday Mass and receiving the sacraments often, and to raise any future children in the Church.[2]

If one of you is Catholic and the other is non-Christian, a dispensation, or exemption from Church law, is required. A marriage between a Catholic and a non-Christian, while it can certainly be loving and fruitful, will be a valid but not sacramental marriage. The reason is that in the Roman rite of the Catholic Church, the couple, not the priest, administers the sacrament of Marriage to each other. Since Baptism is the foundational sacrament, a non-baptized person is not able to give or receive the subsequent sacrament of Matrimony. Although the marriage between a Christian and a non-baptized person is certainly sacred and good, these marriages *can* be "dissolved."[3] In this case, "indissoluble" refers to consummated sacramental marriages. As in the case of marriage between a Catholic Christian and a non-Catholic Christian, the spouse who is Catholic is required to profess that he or she will make efforts to actively practice the Catholic faith and to have children baptized and raised in the Church.

---

2. See Haffner, *The Sacramental Mystery,* 213.
3. Ibid., 215.

In both cases a failure to obtain the required permission or dispensation means that the marriage will not be valid. That is, no marriage, in the eyes of the Church, will occur. These specifications might seem, on the surface, to be fairly harsh when all you want is to spend your life with the person you love. As with any other teaching, though, the Church comes from a place of love. It's wise and prudent to anticipate potential strains on your relationship when deciding how you'll practice your faith as a family. And in a reflection of God's love, the Church only desires to draw souls closer to him. If you esteem the Church enough to get married in it, choosing to pursue that spiritual, divinely blessed bond instead of just a legal piece of paper, it's worth esteeming the Church enough to make the Catholic faith a central part of your life and to bring your children into the body of Christ.

When One or Both of You Have Been Married Before

If a person who has been married before wants to marry again, any previous marriage(s) must be declared null by the Church. Rumor often has it that an annulment is just a Catholic version of divorce, but that's not the case.

A divorce is the legal dissolving of a marriage in the eyes of the state. An annulment, however, is not about the legal aspect but the sacramental. Annulment is based on what actually constitutes a marriage in the eyes of the Church. When a marriage has been *ratified* (that is, the words of the sacrament have been spoken and the couple blessed) and *consummated*, the sacramental reality means that the marriage is literally indissoluble; it can only be broken by death. This is based directly on the words of Christ: "So they are no longer two, but one flesh. Therefore what God has joined together, let no one separate" (Mt 19:6). In other words, it would take more than some divorce paperwork to end such a marriage—you can't dissolve something indissoluble.

Annulment then is not a substitute way to dissolve a marriage. Instead, it means that a marriage (in the sacramental sense of the word) never took place. Jason Evert, a Catholic apologist, explains it like this:

> When two people seek to be united in Christian marriage, certain realities must be present in order for that union to take effect. For example, if one partner is being forced into the marriage, or if one does not intend to be faithful or to be open to children, he or she is not entering what God considers a marriage. Therefore the marriage is not valid. . . . So an annulment does not end a real marriage but declares that there never was a sacramental Marriage to begin with. The Church goes through a long investigation to determine if the marriage was validly contracted. If it was, then even if the marriage turned sour years later, the Church cannot dissolve that. (The couple may separate if necessary, such as in the case of abuse, and even may obtain a civil divorce, but neither is free to remarry.) When a valid marriage has taken place between two baptized persons, only death can sever that bond.[4]

That being said, a holy, sacramental remarriage truly can be an occasion of great joy.

---

4. Catholic Answers, "Isn't an Annulment the Same as a Divorce?" http://chastityproject.com/qa/isnt-an-annulment-the-same-as-a-divorce/.

Appendix C
Wedding Planning Resources, Education and Ministry, and Further Reading

Catholic Wedding Planning and Marriage Prep

A Catholic Handbook for Engaged and Newly Married Couples by Frederick Marks (Steubenville, OH: Emmaus Road Publishing, 2014).

Catholic Marriage Prep (one-on-one Pre-Cana); *www.catholicmarriageprep.com.*

For Your Marriage: An Initiative of the United States Conference of Catholic Bishops; www.foryourmarriage.org.

Pastoral and Matrimonial Renewal Center; *www.pmrcusa.org.*

Together For Life by Joseph M. Champlin and Peter A. Jarret, C.S.C. (Notre Dame, IN: Ave Maria Press, 2012).

Transformed in Love: *Building Your Catholic Marriage* by the Catholic Archdiocese of Boston (Boston: Pauline Books & Media, 2013) (Team Leader Manual and Participant Workbook).

Love, Relationship, and Catholic Marriage

The Five Love Languages by Gary Chapman (Chicago: Northfield Publishing, 2015).

Love and Responsibility by Karol Wojtyla. Translated by Grzegorz Ignatik (Boston: Pauline Books & Media, 2013).

Men, Women, and the Mystery of Love by Edward Sri (Cincinnati: Servant Books, 2007).

A Severe Mercy by Sheldon Vanauken (New York: Harper One, 2009).

Spicing Up Married Life by Rev. Leo Patalinghug (Hunt Valley, MD: Leo McWatkins Films, 2012).

The Temperament God Gave You by Art and Laraine Bennet (Manchester, NH: Sophia Institute Press, 2005).

Three to Get Married by Archbishop Fulton Sheen (New York: Scepter Press, 1996).

Understanding Love and Responsibility by Richard Spinello (Boston: Pauline Books & Media, 2014).

Womanhood and Femininity

By Love Refined: Letters to a Young Bride by Alice von Hildebrand (Manchester, NH: Sophia Institute Press, 1989).

Discovering the Feminine Genius by Katrina Zeno (Boston: Pauline Books & Media, 2010).

ENDOW Ministries; *www.endowgoups.org*.

Made in His Image Ministries; *www.madeinhisimage.org.*

My Peace I Give You: Healing Sexual Wounds with the Help of the Saints by Dawn Eden (Notre Dame, IN: Ave Maria Press, 2012).

On the Dignity and Vocation of Women, Anniversary Edition by John Paul II, with commentary by Genevieve Kineke (Boston: Pauline Books & Media, 2013).

The Thrill of the Chaste by Dawn Eden (Notre Dame, IN: Ave Maria Press, 2015).

Women Made New Ministries; *www.womenmadenew.com.*

Women, Sex, and the Church: A Case for Catholic Teaching Edited by Erika Bachiochi (Boston: Pauline Books & Media, 2010).

Worthy: See Yourself As God Does by Amanda Mortus (Self-published, 2013).

Scripture, Mary, and the Saints

33 Days to Morning Glory by Rev. Michael Gaitley (Stockbridge, MA: Marian Press, 2011).

Bible Basics for Catholics by Louis Bergsma and Scott Hahn (Notre Dame, IN: Ave Maria Press, 2012).

The New Rosary: Biblical Insights for Praying the 20 Mysteries by Edward Sri (Cincinnati: Servant Books, 2011).

The World's First Love: Mary, Mother of God by Archbishop Fulton Sheen (San Francisco: Ignatius Press, 2010).

Masculinity

Be a Man! Becoming the Man God Created You to Be by Rev. Larry Richards (San Francisco: Ignatius Press, 2009).

The King's Men Ministries; *www.thekingsmen.org.*

Man to Man, Dad to Dad: Catholic Faith and Fatherhood edited by Brian Caulfield (Boston: Pauline Books & Media, 2013).

Sexuality

Catholicism and Contraception: What the Church Teaches and Why by Angela Franks (Boston: Pauline Books & Media, 2013).

Chastity Is for Lovers: Single, Happy, and (Still) a Virgin by Arleen Spenceley (Notre Dame, IN: Ave Maria Press, 2014).

Delivered: True Stories of Men and Women Who Turned from Porn to Purity by Matt Fradd (San Diego: Catholic Answers Press, 2014).

Fill These Hearts by Christopher West (New York: Random House, 2012).

Holy Sex by Gregory Popcak (New York: Crossroad, 2008).

Good News about Sex and Marriage: Answers to Your Honest Questions About Catholic Teaching by Christopher West (Cincinnati: Servant Books, 2004).

If You Really Loved Me: 100 Questions on Dating, Relationships, and Sexual Purity by Jason Evert (Cincinnati: Servant Books, 2009).

Man and Woman He Created Them: A Theology of the Body by Pope Saint John Paul II, translated by Michael Waldstein (Boston: Pauline Books & Media, 2006).

Real Love: Answers to Your Questions on Dating, Marriage, and the Real Meaning of Sex by Mary Beth Bonacci (San Francisco: Ignatius Press, 2012).

Theology of the Body for Beginners: An Introduction to Pope Saint John Paul II's Sexual Revolution by Christopher West (West Chester, PA: Ascension Press, 2009).

Natural Family Planning

Did you know there is more than one method of practicing NFP? This section includes resources for the Billings Ovulation Method, Sympto-Thermal Method (through the Couple to Couple League), Creighton Fertility Model, and Marquette Model. The observed signs of fertility and manner of tracking them vary slightly from method to method, yet they are all equally effective. Having multiple options to choose from is helpful because no matter how regular (or irregular) your cycle is or what issues may accompany it, you can find a method that will work for your situation. This section also lists further reading on NFP and medical resources.

Billings Ovulation Method; *http://www.thebillingsovulationmethod. org.*

Couple to Couple League; *http://www.ccli.org.*

Creighton Fertility Model; *http://www.creightonmodel.com.*

Marquette Model; *http://nfp.marquette.edu/..*

NaProTECHNOLOGY for holistic, morally acceptable infertility treatment; *http://www.naprotechnology.com.*

One More Soul NFP Directory and Resources; *http://www.onemoresoul.com.*

The Sinner's Guide to Natural Family Planning by Simcha Fischer (Self-published, 2013).

Appendix D
Sample Invitation and Program Wording

Invitations

Getting married Catholic is unique. You're becoming husband and wife not just legally but also sacramentally. Identifying marriage as a sacrament in your invitation wording reflects that. Feel free to mix and match the word choices in these samples to reflect the family situations and formality of your wedding.

If the bride's parents
are paying for the wedding:

Mr. and Mrs.

_____

Mr. and Mrs. Sanchez

If both sets of parents are
chipping in:

Mr. and Mrs.

_____ &

Mr. and Mrs.

_____

Mr. and Mrs. Oscar Sanchez &
Mr. and Mrs. Mark Jones

If the two of you are paying
for the wedding:

Together with their parents
(*groom's first and last name*)
and (*bride's first and last name*)
request the honor of your
presence at

Together with their parents
María Gonzalez Sanchez
and John Jones
request the honor of your presence at

OR

invite you to celebrate the
marriage of their daughter
(*bride's first and middle name*)
to (*groom's first, middle,
and last name*)

Mr. and Mrs. Sanchez
invite you to celebrate
the marriage of their daughter
María Rosa to
John William Jones

OR

invite you to celebrate the marriage of their children (*bride's first and middle name*) and (*groom's first and middle name*)

> Mr. and Mrs. Sanchez &
> Mr. and Mrs. Jones
> *invite you to celebrate
> the marriage of their children
> María Rosa and John William*

OR

invite you to celebrate the marriage of their children (*bride's first and middle name*) and (*groom's first and middle name*) in the Sacrament of Holy Matrimony

Day of the week, wedding date, and year

Name of the church

Time

Reception to follow

> Mr. and Mrs. Sanchez &
> Mr. and Mrs. Jones
> *invite you to celebrate
> the marriage of their children*
>
> María Rosa and John William
>
> *in the Sacrament of Holy Matrimony
> Saturday, May 5, 2018
> St. Paul's Church
> 10:00 AM*
>
> *Reception to follow*

Reception details are traditionally printed separately from the ceremony invitation and included in the envelope, along with an RSVP card and, if you like, a reply envelope with the return address filled in. To cut down on costs, you can print reception details on the back of the invite (be sure to include the phrase "over" at the bottom of the invitation so guests know there's more information) and skip the return envelope and RSVP cards in favor of an online RSVP. You can set up a reply system on most wedding websites.

Programs

Aside from recognizing the members of your family and wedding party who are sharing in your day, your program serves the added function of guiding your guests through your nuptial Mass. The Mass is the prayer of the Church, so essentially you're inviting your guests to pray with you as you enter into the sacrament.

For guests who aren't Catholic or haven't practiced the faith for a while, attending a Mass can be a powerful experience that engages all the senses: incense, bells, flowers, a beautiful church, and music that lifts the soul. Yet it might also feel long and as if some elements have no rhyme or reason. Here's your chance to explain the practices of the Church, which so often go misunderstood, with charity and clearness.

A sample program order follows, including responses to the prayers of the Mass and guidelines for receiving Communion.

The Nuptial Mass Uniting

(Bride's first, middle, and last name)

and

(Groom's first, middle, and last name)

(optional: in Holy Matrimony)

Date

Name of Church

(optional: city and state)

The Wedding Party

Parents of the Bride
Name and Name

Parents of the Groom
Name and Name

Grandparents of the Bride
Name and Name

Grandparents of the Groom
Name and Name

Maid of Honor
Name

Best Man
Name

Bridesmaids
Name
Name
Name
Name
Name
Name

Groomsmen
Name
Name
Name
Name
Name
Name

Ministers of the Liturgy

Celebrant

The priest's name

Concelebrants

(any other priests who will be celebrating the Mass)

Names

Deacon(s)

Names

Altar Servers

Name

Name

Readers

Name

Name

Extraordinary Ministers of the Eucharist

Name

Name

Musicians

Name

Name

Order of Worship

ENTRANCE RITE

Processional

(Processional song and name of composer)

(Song for the entrance of the bride and name of composer)

PENITENTIAL RITE

Opening Prayer

Please be seated.

LITURGY OF THE WORD

FIRST READING

From the Book of _____ (chapter and verses)

(Include the text of the first reading here)

The Word of the Lord.
Response: **Thanks be to God.**

Responsorial Psalm

Response: (include the text of the Psalm response here.)

SECOND READING

From the (First, Second) Letter of _____ (to the _____)
chapter and verses

(Include the text of the second reading here)

The Word of the Lord.

Response: **Thanks be to God.**

Gospel Acclamation
Please stand.

GOSPEL

According to _____ chapter and verses

(Include the text of the Gospel here)

The Gospel of the Lord.

Response: **Praise to you, Lord Jesus Christ.**

Homily

RITE OF MARRIAGE

Statement of Intentions

Consent and Exchange of Vows

Blessing and Exchange of Rings

Prayer of the Faithful

LITURGY OF THE EUCHARIST

Presentation and Preparation of the Gifts
   (Song selection and name of composer; if you like, you can also include the lyrics.)

Holy, Holy
Please kneel.

Memorial Acclamation

Great Amen
Please stand.

The Lord's Prayer

Nuptial Blessing

Lamb of God

   (You might like to include these guidelines from the USCCB.)

Guidelines for Receiving Communion

For Catholics

   As Catholics, we fully participate in the celebration of the Eucharist when we receive Holy Communion. We are encouraged to receive Communion devoutly and frequently. In order to be properly disposed to receive Communion, participants should not be conscious of grave sin and normally should have fasted for one hour. A person who is conscious of grave sin is not to receive the Body and Blood of the Lord without prior sacramental confession except for a grave reason where there is no opportunity for confession. In this case, the person is to be mindful of the obligation to make an act of perfect contrition, including the intention of confessing as soon as possible (canon 916). A frequent reception of the sacrament of Penance is encouraged for all.

For Our Fellow Christians

We welcome our fellow Christians to this celebration of the Eucharist as our brothers and sisters. We pray that our common baptism and the action of the Holy Spirit in this Eucharist will draw us closer to one another and begin to dispel the sad divisions which separate us. We pray that these will lessen and finally disappear, in keeping with Christ's prayer for us "that they may all be one" (Jn 17:21).

Because Catholics believe that the celebration of the Eucharist is a sign of the reality of the oneness of faith, life, and worship, members of those churches with whom we are not yet fully united are ordinarily not admitted to Holy Communion. Eucharistic sharing in exceptional circumstances by other Christians requires permission according to the directives of the diocesan bishop and the provisions of canon law (canon 844 §4). Members of the Orthodox Churches, the Assyrian Church of the East, and the Polish National Catholic Church are urged to respect the discipline of their own Churches. According to Roman Catholic discipline, the Code of Canon Law does not object to the reception of Communion by Christians of these Churches (canon 844 §3).

For Those Not Receiving Holy Communion

All who are not receiving Holy Communion are encouraged to express in their hearts a prayerful desire for unity with the Lord Jesus and with one another.

For Non-Christians

We also welcome to this celebration those who do not share our faith in Jesus Christ. While we cannot admit them to Holy Communion, we ask them to offer their prayers for the peace and the unity of the human family.

— *United States Conference of Catholic Bishops*

(Or you might prefer to use a shorter, paraphrased version, like the following:)

Catholics believe that the Eucharist is the Body, Blood, Soul and Divinity of Jesus Christ. When we receive Communion, we enter into an intimate, living union with Christ. The Eucharist is the source and summit of the Catholic faith, uniting the entire Church in faith and worship.

Catholics who are sacramentally prepared for Communion (that is, they are not conscious of grave sin) are invited to receive. Those who are not receiving Holy Communion (including non-Catholics) are encouraged to express in their hearts a prayerful sense of unity and are invited to come forward for a blessing with arms crossed over their chest.

Communion

(Song selection title and name of composer; if you like, you can also include the lyrics.)

Dedication to the Blessed Mother

(Song selection title and name of composer)

CONCLUDING RITE

Solemn Blessing

Recessional

(Song selection and name of composer; if you like, you can also include the lyrics.)

(If you like, conclude your program with a note to your guests expressing your gratitude for forming you into the people you've become and for sharing in the celebration of your marriage.)

You might also include:

In Memoriam

(List the names of any deceased family members or friends who could not attend)

(A favorite Scripture passage or quote.)

The back page of your program is a perfect, convenient spot to print directions to the reception!

BOOKS & MEDIA

The Daughters of St. Paul operate book and media centers at the following addresses. Visit, call, or write the one nearest you today, or find us at www.pauline.org.

CALIFORNIA

3908 Sepulveda Blvd, Culver City, CA 90230	310-397-8676
935 Brewster Avenue, Redwood City, CA 94063	650-369-4230
5945 Balboa Avenue, San Diego, CA 92111	858-565-9181

FLORIDA

145 S.W. 107th Avenue, Miami, FL 33174	305-559-6715

HAWAII

1143 Bishop Street, Honolulu, HI 96813	808-521-2731

ILLINOIS

172 North Michigan Avenue, Chicago, IL 60601	312-346-4228

LOUISIANA

4403 Veterans Memorial Blvd, Metairie, LA 70006	504-887-7631

MASSACHUSETTS

885 Providence Hwy, Dedham, MA 02026	781-326-5385

MISSOURI

9804 Watson Road, St. Louis, MO 63126	314-965-3512

NEW YORK

64 W. 38th Street, New York, NY 10018	212-754-1110

SOUTH CAROLINA

243 King Street, Charleston, SC 29401	843-577-0175

TEXAS

Currently no book center; for parish exhibits or outreach evangelization, contact: 210-569-0500, or SanAntonio@paulinemedia.com, or P.O. Box 761416, San Antonio, TX 78245

VIRGINIA

1025 King Street, Alexandria, VA 22314	703-549-3806

CANADA

3022 Dufferin Street, Toronto, ON M6B 3T5	416-781-9131